RED SKY AT NIGHT

THE BOOK OF LOST COUNTRYSIDE WISDOM

Jane Struthers

EBURY
PRESS

First published in 2009 by Ebury Press, an imprint of Ebury Publishing
A Random House Group company

The Random House Group Limited Reg. No. 954009

Addresses for companies within the Random House Group can be found at
www.randomhouse.co.uk

A CIP catalogue record for this book is available from the British Library

The Random House Group Limited supports The Forest Stewardship
Council (FSC), the leading international forest certification organisation.
All our titles that are printed on Greenpeace approved FSC certified paper
carry the FSC logo. Our paper procurement policy can be
found at www.rbooks.co.uk/environment

Mixed Sources
Product group from well-managed
forests and other controlled sources
www.fsc.org Cert no. TT-COC-2139
© 1996 Forest Stewardship Council

FSC

Printed in the UK by CPI Mackays, Chatham, ME5 8TD

ISBN 9780091932442

To buy books by your favourite authors and register for offers visit
www.rbooks.co.uk

In memory of Bert Tanner, my great-uncle and godfather,
who loved the countryside

CONTENTS

THE STARRY HEAVENS

SNUG INDOORS

IN THE KITCHEN

A WELL STOCKED LARDER

THE TURNING OF THE YEAR

FOREWORD

> When two Englishmen meet, their first
> talk is of the weather.
>
> DR SAMUEL JOHNSON

Britain has many traditions, but this is one of the most sacrosanct. How else can we get through those awkward silences that have a habit of springing up? Besides, the weather changes so frequently in Britain that there is usually something to say about it. Most of us rely on official weather forecasts to tell us what to expect, but in the days before television, radio and even newspapers, it was essential to be able to predict the weather oneself. Farmers, sailors and other people whose livelihoods – and possibly even their lives – depended on the weather were expert at reading the sky and noticing other indications of changing conditions.

Today, the ability to predict the weather by sniffing the air, looking at the clouds and observing the activity of insects is fast disappearing. Our lives are so hectic that we often don't have the time to notice what's going on around us. Many other aspects of country knowledge are being lost, too, as we become more disconnected from our surroundings.

Red Sky at Night is rich in the countryside wisdom that once we knew so well. It's a miscellany of information about the countryside and its lore, from the sensible to the fanciful, from the superstitious to the factual, that was once common knowledge but is now being forgotten. Here are the notions, beliefs, rules and facts that our fore-fathers lived by. They offer a link to a way of life that's gentle, measured, and governed by the rhythms of the seasons and the turning points of the year. They include recipes, instructions, lists, collections, stories, histories, ideas, calendars, traditions and many other things that I hope will inspire you, make you think or conjure up fascinating images of a lost world.

Jane Struthers
East Sussex
St David's Day 2009

ALL CREATURES GREAT AND SMALL

Animals are such agreeable friends – they ask no questions, they pass no criticisms.

'MR GILFIL'S LOVE STORY', GEORGE ELIOT

WHAT DO YOU CALL A ...?

Some animals have special names, according to whether they're male, female or very young. So if you don't know that a tercel or a squab is, this is your chance to find out.

Animal	Male	Female	Young
Badger	Boar	Sow	Kit, cub
Bat	Male	Female	Pup
Bee	Drone	Queen, worker	Larva
Bird	Cock	Hen	Chick
Boar	Boar	Sow	Farrow
Cat	Tom	Queen	Kitten
Cattle	Bull	Cow	Calf
Chicken	Rooster	Hen	Chick
Deer	Buck, stag	Doe, hind	Faun
Dog	Dog	Bitch	Puppy, whelp
Donkey	Jackass	Jenny	Colt, foal
Duck	Drake	Duck	Duckling
Falcon	Tercel	Falcon	Eyas, chick
Ferret	Hob	Jill	Kit
Fox	Dog	Vixen	Cub
Frog	Male	Female	Tadpole
Goat	Billy	Nanny	Kid
Goose	Gander	Goose	Gosling
Hare	Buck, jack	Doe, jill	Leveret
Hawk	Tercel	Haggard	Eyas, chick
Hedgehog	Male	Female	Hoglet
Horse	Stallion	Mare	Foal
Mink	Boar	Sow	Cub
Mouse	Buck	Doe	Pup
Peafowl	Peacock	Peahen	Peachick
Pig	Boar	Sow	Piglet

Animal	Male	Female	Young
Pigeon	Cock	Hen	Squab
Porpoise	Bull	Cow	Calf
Rabbit	Buck	Doe	Bunny
Rat	Buck	Doe	Pup
Seal	Bull	Cow	Pup
Sheep	Ram	Ewe	Lamb
Spider	Male	Female	Spiderling
Squirrel	Buck	Doe	Pup
Swan	Cob	Pen	Cygnet
Turkey	Tom	Hen	Poult
Weasel	Jack	Jill	Kit

As mad as a March hare . . .

If you've heard the phrase 'mad as a March hare', you may have wondered what it means. What exactly are March hares, and why are they mad?

∽ Boxing matches ∽

Hares are a fairly rare sight in the British countryside, although that might be because from a distance they can be confused with rabbits.

But not so each March and April, when hares behave in ways that have led to them affectionately being labelled as mad. That's because each spring, in addition to chasing one another and leaping around, hares have boxing matches with each other. There is some debate about whether it is only male hares (bucks) that do this, or whether female hares (does) join in as well. Originally, boxing hares were thought to be two bucks sparring over a doe, but it is now believed they involve a doe fending off the unwanted advances of a buck because she isn't yet ready to mate with him. Perhaps this is her way of hitting her unwelcome admirer round the head with her handbag.

❦ Types of British hare ❦

There are two breeds of hare in Britain. The brown hare (*Lepus europaeus*) occupies lowland areas of arable land and open grassland in England, Wales and Scotland, but is very rarely seen in Ireland. These animals are active during the morning and evening, but literally lie low during the day – they like to stretch out in fields, with their ears laid flat along their backs, in shallow depressions known as forms. They have brown coats, long ears (much longer than a rabbit's) with black tips, and long back legs.

The mountain or blue hare (*Lepus timidus*) lives in the Scottish Highlands, keeping well out of the way of potential predators such as eagles. This hare's coat changes colour according to the season: it's brown in the summer, white in the winter to provide camouflage against the snow, and bluish in the spring and autumn because the brown of the summer coat mingles with the white of its winter fur.

BEE LORE

Bees are among the busiest creatures in our gardens and in the wild, and also some of the most important because they pollinate so many plants. In years gone by, many gardeners kept their own beehives, which provided a welcome supply of honey that could be used in many different ways. For instance, the honey was eaten and the wax coating on the combs was made into candles. In return, there was a strict etiquette in looking after bees and many people still practise it, with excellent results.

✺ Informing the bees ✺

Bees were once often referred to as 'little servants of God' or 'small messengers of God', names which meant they had to be accorded due respect. One of the most important tasks of any beekeeper was to keep his or her bees informed of the latest news, because they were part of the family and it was only polite to keep them up to date. If someone died, the bees had to be told, often by someone tapping gently on their hive with a front-door key and then explaining what had happened. If you failed to tell the bees about a death, the penalties could be severe. At the very least, the hive might swarm and vanish. Much worse, there might be another death in the family. In some parts of the country, the hive was draped in black crêpe to signify mourning.

But bees weren't only told about the bad news. They were also informed when there was something to celebrate, such as a wedding or christening, and a small slice of the cake would be left outside their hive for them to feed on. Some people also tied a white ribbon to the hive. Once again, the consequences of failing to notify the bees were serious. The bees might fly away, or bad luck might befall the family. If the bees weren't told about the birth of a child, there was a danger that the child might sicken or even die. The bees might follow suit, through grief at not being kept up to date with the family news.

✺ Humming ✺

The noise that the bees made was highly significant. Silence from the hive was a warning that the bees might soon swarm. On the other hand, if there was a contented buzzing, all was well. It was considered highly inadvisable to swear near the hive, in case you offended the bees and they abandoned the hive in disgust. If you had to move the hive, it was wise to avoid doing so on Good Friday, once again for fear of upsetting the bees.

⮞ Acquiring the bees ⮜

How did you acquire your hive in the first place? You had to do it tactfully, so as not to hurt the bees' feelings. It wasn't a good idea to buy the bees, but if you had no choice, it was advisable to hand over the money (usually a gold coin) discreetly, well away from the hive. Better still was to exchange the hive for something useful, such as some wheat. But not even the wisest precautions were any good if the bees weren't told they were going to have a new master or mistress. Such a lack of consideration could result in the death of the bees. You might think this practice has long since died out, but in fact it's still performed in some parts of the countryside. And according to the people who take care of their bees in this way, it works perfectly.

WHICH FLOWERS MAKE
THE BEST HONEY?

Bees take the pollen from all sorts of different flowers and plants to make honey, with varying results. Some flowers make much nicer honey than others. For instance, it is claimed that honey made from oil seed rape is bitter and highly crystallised. Here are some good varieties to try.

Type of honey	Taste	Colour
Acacia blossom	Lightly floral and sweet	White to light amber
Clover	Delicate	White to light amber
Heather	Floral, with a strong flavour and aftertaste	Dark amber
Lavender	Lavender	Mid amber
Orange blossom	Fragrantly citrus	Light to dark amber
Rosemary	Herby	Light amber
Thyme	Herby	Dark amber
Wildflowers	Depends on the mix	Medium amber

THE LIFE OF A BUTTERFLY

Of all the insects, butterflies and moths go through the most remarkable transformations in their relatively short lives. If they were ever to have family reunions it's highly unlikely that they would recognise one another because they undergo four very different stages during their existence. It puts an entirely new spin on those irritating words so often uttered by older relatives to small children, such as 'My, how you've changed! I wouldn't have known you.'

❦ The egg ❦

The first stage for a butterfly or moth is when a female lays her eggs. These are sticky, so they will adhere to the specific form of plant life best suited to the needs of the larva (better known as the caterpillar) that emerges. Unless the species is the type whose eggs overwinter, this egg stage only lasts about one week before the caterpillar develops.

☙ The caterpillar ❧

The caterpillar's main aim is to feed, so it can store as much energy as possible to sustain it through its next stage. This is why caterpillars can be such a menace in the garden, such as the caterpillars of the cabbage white butterfly, which have such a fondness for our carefully nurtured brassicas. During this stage, the caterpillar undergoes a series of stages that are called instars. It moults towards the end of each instar, shedding its old cuticle and growing a new one. It also begins the slow process of growing wing discs that will eventually turn into the proper wings of a butterfly. At the time of the final instar, these wing discs become much bigger and more developed.

☙ The pupa ❧

After about one month, when all these instars have been completed, the caterpillar is ready to move on to the next stage. It finds somewhere safe in which to hide, sometimes attaching itself to a plant stem, while it forms a pupa (also known as a chrysalis). After a few days, the caterpillar's skin dries out and falls off, revealing the chrysalis. If you look at it closely, you can see the outlines of the butterfly's eyes, tongue, legs and wings. Although it may seem inert, a complete transformation is taking place inside the chrysalis.

☙ The butterfly ❧

When everything is ready, after between two and three weeks of pupation, the chrysalis splits and the nascent butterfly wriggles free. It perches on a leaf or twig to wait while its wings dry and expand,

and the blood begins to flow through them properly. It is then ready to fly, to feed on nectar through its long, tube-like tongue and, most importantly, to mate so the entire process can start again.

HORSE TALK

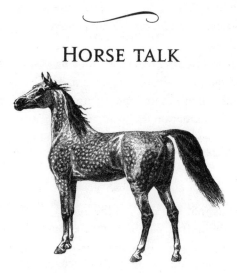

The world of horses has its own complex language which you need to master if you want to tell your dam from your dray. Even the colours of horses' coats require a special vocabulary.

❧ Colours ❧

Describing the colour of a horse's coat is a lot more complicated than it first seems. Here are some of the most common colours, although there are many more.

Bay   Red-brown body with black 'points' (black mane, tail and lower legs, and black tips of the ears). The variations within this category include light bay (light red coat), blood bay (bright red coat) and dark bay (very dark red or brown). Whatever the colour of the coat, a bay always has black points.

Chestnut Reddish coat, with the mane and tail the same colour or lighter. Variations include sorrel (coppery red) and liver chestnut or brown (very dark brown coat).

Grey White, or black and white, coat with a dark skin, especially noticeable around the eyes and muzzle. The coat will lighten with age.

Palomino Yellow, tan or golden coat with a pale blond or white mane and tail.

Roan White hairs intermingled with those of any other dark colour, except on the head, mane, tail and lower legs. The coat does not lighten with age.

➳ Age ➳

Tradition tells us that you can tell the age of a horse by looking at its teeth – assuming that you feel brave enough. Luckily, this isn't always necessary. Horses that take part in competitions in the northern hemisphere are considered to become one year older each 1 January (which means they're all honorary Capricorns). So even if a horse is only six months old on 1 January it's considered to be one year old from that date. Horses competing in the southern hemisphere have another year added to their age each 1 August (so they're all honorary Leos). The only exception to this rule is in endurance riding (a long-distance sport) in which the horse's exact age is used.

Horses are given different names according to their age, and also according to the sport in which they may be involved.

Foal A horse of either sex less than twelve months old.

Yearling A horse of either sex between one and two years old.

Colt A male horse less than four years old. (British horseracing extends this to five years old.)

Filly A female horse less than four years old. (British horseracing extends this to five years old.)

Stallion   A non-castrated male horse over four years old.
Gelding   A castrated male horse over four years old.
Mare   A female horse over four years old.

➤ Horseracing ➤

There are two main types of horseracing in Britain, each of which has its own racecourses.

Flat races   Races run on a level surface, at distances varying from 5 furlongs (1,006 m) to more than 2 miles (3,219 m). These are divided into two categories:
    Conditions races – classic and local races.
    Handicap races – daily races in which horses are given handicaps (weights to carry) according to their abilities.

National Hunt races   Races in which horses have to jump hurdles or fences (may also be referred to as steeplechasing). Occasionally there are also National Hunt flat (or bumper) races in which jump horses are trained to race one another on a level surface before beginning their careers as National Hunt horses.

WHEN IS A MULE NOT A MULE?

Strictly speaking, a mule isn't a mule when it's a hinny. But what is a mule in the first place? And what, then, is a hinny?

A mule is the hybrid animal produced when a male donkey (a jackass) mates with a female horse (a mare). A hinny, on the other hand, is the product of a male horse (a stallion) mating with a female donkey (a jenny). Hinnies are more rare than mules.

Mules and hinnies are usually sterile because of a discrepancy between the number of chromosomes in horses and donkeys: horses have sixty-four chromosomes but donkeys have only sixty-two. When a male donkey does successfully mate with a female horse (at which point she is referred to as a 'molly'), each resulting mule has sixty-three chromosomes.

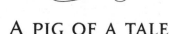

A PIG OF A TALE

Although the fourteen pedigree breeds of pigs in Britain include breeds that originated in other parts of the world, some traditional breeds are thoroughly British. Sadly, some have been lost completely, not least because of government policies that deliberately reduced what was then a healthy diversity of pig breeds into only three breeds (the Large White, Landrace and Welsh) or, as was preferred, a single type of pig that would be suitable for commercial production. Among the breeds that were lost for ever were the Cumberland, the Dorset Gold Tip, the Lincolnshire Curly Coated, the Ulster White and the Yorkshire Blue. The Essex Saddleback and the Wessex Saddleback were crossed to create a new breed known as the British Saddleback. For a while, it looked as though the other traditional breeds would go the same way but, happily, their decline is now slowly being reversed although they are still considered to be at risk.

Here are some of them, in all their glory.

⁓ Berkshire ⁓

This is a traditional British pig although, as a result of cross-breeding with Chinese and Siamese breeds, the Cromwellian soldiers who enjoyed eating its bacon during the English Civil War would no longer recognise it. Today's Berkshire has black skin, white socks and pricked-up ears.

⁓ British Saddleback ⁓

This is a relatively new breed, created in 1967 by crossing the Essex and Wessex Saddlebacks. It has black skin and lop ears, with a white band that encompasses the area around its front legs and shoulders. The sows are known to make good mothers and are very hardy, so they enjoy the outdoor life.

⁓ Gloucestershire Old Spot ⁓

Of all the pedigree pigs, this is the breed that has become best known in recent years. As its name implies, it is noted for its big, black splotches, which stand out on its white body. These pigs have always been popular in Gloucestershire, where they once liked to graze in apple orchards, snuffling up all the windfalls. They are resilient and hardy, and are happiest living outdoors.

⁓ Large Black ⁓

This breed has the distinction of being the only all-black pig in Britain. It has lop ears and is another very hardy creature. What's more, the sows make excellent mothers. Although the fashion for coloured pigs has declined in recent years, the Large Black's exceptional meat means it's once again bred for its eating qualities.

⁓ Middle White ⁓

The Middle White is an offshoot of the Large White breed, and was only recognised as such in 1852 when judges at a Yorkshire agricultural show noticed that some of the pigs seemed smaller than the rest. However, they weren't so small that they belonged to the Small White breed, and so they were named the Middle Breed. They make good eating and in the early 20th century were popularly known as the 'London Porker'. Although they declined in popularity later in the century, they are once again highly valued for their meat. Several chefs claim that the Middle White makes the best crackling.

❧ Oxford Sandy and Black ❧

This breed, sometimes known as the 'Plum Pudding Pig' because of its random black splotches on a sandy skin, was once a particular favourite of cottagers and farmers and is thought to have existed for at least two hundred years. Despite this claim to fame, it nearly became extinct in the 20th century, but its numbers are slowly starting to increase again.

❧ Tamworth ❧

With its pricked-up ears and long snout, the Tamworth bears the closest resemblance to the Old English Forest Pig from which it has descended. It has a pink skin with sandy-gold hair, and has an inquisitive nature. It likes the outdoor life and was often kept by cottagers, especially in the Midlands. When its numbers looked dangerously close to extinction from the 1970s onwards, several boars were imported from Australia for breeding purposes. The breed became world-famous in 1998 when two pigs (dubbed the 'Tamworth Two' by the press, and later named Butch and Sundance) escaped while being herded into an abattoir and lived on the run for a week before being tracked down. Luckily for them, they were sent to spend the rest of their lives at the Rare Breeds Centre in Kent.

❧ Welsh ❧

These pigs have long lop ears, pink skin and long bodies. Their numbers soared in the period immediately after the Second World

War, making them one of the most popular pig breeds in Britain. Today, they are popular for cross-breeding, and do well whether living in indoor or outdoor conditions.

THE LIFECYCLE OF FROGS

I f you have ever heard the Hungarian marsh frog in full cry on the Kent/East Sussex border, you will know what a racket a frog can make. It's extraordinary that so much noise can come out of such a small body. Yet all frogs are remarkable, because of their lifecycle. Like butterflies and moths, they undergo an astonishing metamorphosis in order to reach adulthood.

☙ The egg ❧

Each frog begins life as a single egg that is laid by its mother in a huge mass of thousands of other eggs. Every egg has the potential to develop into a frog, but there are so many predators looking on it as a nice snack that it's quite likely to be eaten. Luckily, nature has taken care of this by giving each egg a few advantages. One is that each egg is black, which enables it to absorb more heat from the sun and therefore to develop more quickly. The sheer number of eggs laid at any one time also contributes to the survival rate, because it's unlikely that they will all be eaten, and the jelly that surrounds each egg is another factor in its potential survival. Some species of frog lay eggs that are poisonous to any creature that tries to eat them.

⇜ The tadpole ⇝

Assuming that the egg survives this first stage, it begins to develop into a tiny tadpole within one to three weeks. For most species, this means that it starts to grow a tail, has eyes (but no eyelids), forms a mouth and develops external gills. At this stage, the tadpole may eat the algae in the water, although some species are carnivorous.

⇜ The frog ⇝

The next stage sees the tadpole metamorphose into a frog. Between six and nine weeks after it emerged from its egg, the tadpole begins to look more recognisable as a frog. It gradually develops miniature front and hind legs, it reabsorbs its tail, loses its external gills, grows eyelids for eyes that change their shape and position on its face, and grows internal lungs. Its diet alters, too, as it switches from being herbivorous to carnivorous.

⇜ Mating rituals ⇝

Generally speaking, when it's time to mate, frogs like to return to the same stretch of water in which they were born, although this doesn't always happen. At mating time, the male frog mounts the female and clasps her body in what is called the amplexus position. He can stay in this position for days at a time, fertilising the eggs as she lays them. And it's at this point that the whole cycle starts again.

OH! DEER!

One of the joys of getting out into the countryside in Britain is seeing the deer. They mostly live in woodland, which offers them plenty of cover. There are six species of deer now living in Britain, although three of them have only been introduced during the past hundred years. Confusingly, the terminology for male, female and young deer changes according to the species.

❧ Chinese water deer (*Hydropotes inermis*) ❧

Although they are between the roe and muntjac deer in size, there is no mistaking the Chinese water deer because of their large, round ears and, in adult bucks, their tusks. They don't have antlers, unlike other deer, and the existence of the tusks indicates that they're a very primitive species of deer. Their coats are reddish-brown in summer and fade to a greyish-brown in winter. The first members of this species arrived in London Zoo in 1873, and more were introduced to Whipsnade Zoo in 1929 but some of these escaped into the wild. Chinese water deer are a solitary species outside the rutting season, which lasts from November to December. The does (females) normally give birth to between one and three fauns (their young), although it has been known for them to have six fauns in a litter.

❧ Fallow deer (*Dama dama*) ❧

Like so many other things in Britain, these deer came over with the Normans after the Norman Conquest. With their delicate appearance and white-spotted, chestnut summer coats, fallow deer are very attractive. The bucks (males) sport antlers that are broad and spatulate. The does give birth to their fauns between May and June. They live in large, single-sex herds in forests and woodland for most of the year and only mix with the opposite sex during the rutting season each autumn. They like to keep on the move and can do lots of damage to trees by nibbling the bark. Being quite tame, these deer can become semi-domesticated.

❧ Muntjac deer (*Muntiacus reevsi*) ❧

Most definitely not a native of Britain, the muntjac was introduced from China to the parkland at Woburn Park in Bedfordshire in the early 20th century. It soon spread into the wild, partly through deliberate releases from a variety of locations and also when some of the deer made a successful bid for freedom. Muntjac deer have long, pointed muzzles and big, spoon-like ears. Their coats are russet in the summer and grey in the winter. Most notably, they look hunched because their haunches (hind legs) are longer than their withers (front legs). When disturbed, the bucks bark and the does and kids (their young) squeak. They like living in forests although they have been known to settle in gardens, too. Instead of having a defined breeding season, muntjac breed throughout the year.

✎ Red deer (*Cervus elaphus*) ✎

This is the largest species of deer (as well as the largest land mammal in Britain). As its name implies, the red deer has a reddish coat although this is only in the summer (it becomes lighter in the winter). The stags (males) grow very large, multi-branched antlers each spring and shed them each winter. The hinds (females) give birth to a single calf (young) each June or thereabouts. Red deer are social animals and live in groups for most of the year. They like to live in woodland, although the gradual decline of their favoured habitat has led to them having to adapt to living in conditions that are more open. They're particularly prevalent in Scotland.

Roe deer (*Capreolus capreolus*)

Roe deer had become extinct in England by the 18th century, although they survived in small pockets of the Scottish Highlands, but they have since been reintroduced into the wild. Roe deer have rich, red coats in summer and grey ones, with yellow spots, in winter. They live mostly in woodland although they can live in areas that are more open, too. The bucks have short antlers with six sharp points. The does give birth to their kids in May or June, and they often have twins and sometimes even triplets. The does often leave their kids hidden in long grass while they graze nearby, returning to suckle their young several times a day.

Sika deer (*Cervus nippon*)

This deer is another introduction from the Far East, and first arrived in Britain in 1860 when one stag and three hinds were introduced to a deer park in Eniskerry, Eire. It's believed that almost all the sika now living in England and Scotland are direct descendants from those original deer. In summer, sika deer have reddish-brown coats, with a dark dorsal stripe surrounded by white spots. In the winter, the spots fade or vanish and the coat becomes grey or black. The stags have branched antlers that are similar to those of the red deer, but with no more than eight points. The rutting season is between late September and November. Sika deer are very vocal, with a wide range of different calls.

GOING BATS

Bats often get a bad press, considered to be scary things that get caught up in your hair or relieve you of several pints of blood each night. The truth is very different, because bats are miraculous creatures that help to keep down the populations of such summer pests as mosquitoes and midges. Even a common pipistrelle

(*Pipistrellus pipistrellus*) can eat over three thousand tiny insects in a night, which is good news because it means they won't be eating you.

⇜ Navigating in the dark ⇝

It's often assumed that bats are blind, but this is wrong. They can see perfectly well but they fly around at night and therefore need to know where they're going. In order to do this, they use something called echolocation, which measures the length of time it takes for the echoes of their calls to be bounced back to them. Each species of bat has its own frequency of calls, which is one of the ways of identifying them if you have a special bat detector. Their calls are often emitted at a frequency that's too high for the human ear to hear.

⇜ Some different species ⇝

There are seventeen different species of bat living in the UK, some of which are much more rare than others. The common pipistrelle and the soprano pipistrelle (*Pipistrellus pygmaeus*) are the most widespread species, although the brown long-eared bat (*Plecotus auritus*) is also quite common. Bechstein's bat (*Myotis bechsteini*) is very rare, and the greater mouse-eared bat (*Myotis myotis*) is almost extinct.

Many bats like to live in buildings, including churches and houses, and the law protects them from interference by humans. Unlike rodents, which chew through wires and wood, bats do no harm to the buildings in which they roost.

WHEN THE WILD WOLVES WENT

Wild wolves are now extinct in Britain, although you can visit some packs living in captivity to see how beautiful they are. There are also tentative moves to reintroduce some wolves to northern Scotland, which is ironic considering the harsh fate that these animals suffered in Britain during the past thousand years.

The wolves that once freely roamed the British countryside never stood a chance, having been hunted and killed as dangerous vermin for centuries. They were regarded with fear and disgust, and many people thought that the sooner they were exterminated the better.

❧ Early respect for wolves ❧

For centuries, wild grey wolves (*Canis lupus*) roamed around Britain. They were definitely an important feature of Anglo-Saxon life (in other words, before the Norman Conquest of 1066) because their bones have been discovered in archaeological excavations and many Anglo-Saxon place names included 'wulf', which was their word for a wolf. The Suffolk village that's now known as Wolfpit was listed as 'Wlfpeta' in the Domesday Book and is believed to be a corruption of Wolfpit. Other place names with a lupine connection include Wolfsdale in Pembrokeshire and Wolfhill in Perth and Kinross. A jewel-encrusted purse found at the Sutton Hoo excavation in Suffolk was decorated with images of wolves, which suggests at the very least a sense of respect for these creatures.

❧ Death to all wolves ❧

The Anglo-Saxons may have honoured the presence of wolves but the Norman invaders certainly didn't. William the Conqueror and his Norman successors paid people to hunt and kill wolves, and they also handed out handsome bounties to any villager who caught and killed a wolf. At a time of financial hardship for many people, this must have been a very tempting incentive.

The wolves' days were numbered and they started to die out. There is no mention of them in Wales after 1166, but they were still living in the Welsh Marches (the area between the Principality of Wales and England) and the adjacent English counties. Not for long, however, because in 1281 Edward I ordered the wholesale slaughter of every wolf in England. He also encouraged coppicing because it was said to keep 'wolves and other malefactors' at bay, and this was practised especially in the Forest of Dean in Gloucestershire. Edward's instructions sounded the death knell for English wolves. He is popularly known as the 'Hammer of the Scots' because of his aggressive warfare with them, but clearly he wasn't good news for wolves either.

Successive kings wanted to make sure that no wolves had survived in England, so noblemen were often paid to kill any wolves that they saw. It was an effective policy and ensured that English wolves had become extinct by the late 15th century.

❧ The fate of Scottish wolves ❧

Scotland was a separate country from England during the medieval period but for centuries it pursued its own anti-wolf policy with vigour, with many laws passed on the subject. Wolves and other wild animals were often hunted and killed for sport: for instance, in 1528 the Earl of Atholl organised a hunt of 'wolff, fox and wild cattis' in honour of James V of Scotland.

The wolves retreated to the north of Scotland, taking refuge in the vast highland forests that then covered thousands of acres of land. But their hunters followed, and often cleared areas of trees in order to expose the animals and reduce their shelter. It was only a matter of time before the wolves died out. No one knows exactly when it happened, although various people claimed – all at different times – to have killed 'the last wolf in Scotland'.

∾ Irish wolves ∾

It was the same story in Ireland, where wolves once roamed freely but were eventually persecuted and hunted into extinction. There was a flurry of anti-wolf legislation in the 1650s, and high bounties for the corpses encouraged people to kill any wolves that they saw. There were reports of wolves still being killed in County Cork in the early 1700s, but the few remaining Irish animals were killed in County Wicklow in the mid 1700s. When they died, the British wolf population was finally extinguished.

BIRDS OF A FEATHER

The pious bird with the scarlet breast
Our little English robin.

'THE REDBREAST CHASING THE BUTTERFLY',
WILLIAM WORDSWORTH

An Aviary of Birds

You might have heard of a gaggle of geese, but what do you call a group of ducks? Or ravens? Here are sixty of the best collective nouns for groups of particular birds.

A bevy of quail

A bevy of swans

A bouquet of pheasants (when flushed)

A building of rooks

A cast of falcons

A charm of finches

A chattering of choughs

A clutter of starlings

A confusion of guinea fowl

A congregation of plovers

A convocation of eagles

A covey of grouse

A covey of partridges

A covey of ptarmigans

A covey of quail

A deceit of lapwings

A descent of woodpeckers

A dole of doves

A dropping of pigeons

An exaltation of larks

A fall of woodcocks

A flight of cormorants

A flight of goshawks

A flight of swallows

A gaggle of geese

A hedge of herons

A herd of wrens

A kettle of hawks

A murder of crows

A muster of storks

A nye of pheasants (while on the ground)

An ostentation of peacocks

A paddling of ducks (while swimming)

A parliament of owls

A parliament of rooks

A party of jays

A peep of chickens

A piteousness of doves

A pitying of turtledoves

A plump of wildfowl

A quarrel of sparrows

A raft of ducks (while idle in water)

A raft of widgeon

A rafter of turkeys

A richness of martins

A scold of jays

A sedge of bitterns

A siege of cranes

A skein of geese (in flight)

A sord of mallards

A spring of teal

A team of ducks (on the wing)

A tidings of magpies

A tok of capercailzies

A train of jackdaws

A trip of dotterel

An unkindness of ravens

A wake of vultures

A watch of nightingales

A wisp of snipe

STRICTLY FOR THE BIRDS

Spurred on by worrying stories about the decline of some of our native birds, many of us are tempted to feed the birds that visit our gardens. But what should we give them to help them survive in the wild? Some of the traditional foods that are put out for birds, such as breadcrumbs, aren't as good for them as you might think. For instance, you should never put out large pieces of nut in the summer months, in case young birds choke on them. Here are some suggestions for foods that will keep birds healthy as well as encourage them back into your garden day after day.

✎ Fat balls ✎

Why spend lots of money buying these when you can easily make your own? Put them out in the winter when birds need the extra energy that comes from saturated fat. A suitable proportion is one-third of suet or lard to two-thirds of the other ingredients, such as chopped cheese, stale cake, chopped nuts, dried fruit and uncooked oatmeal. Melt the fat, stir in the dry ingredients and mix them together. You can either squish this mixture into an empty coconut shell that you hang from a tree or put wedges of the fatty mixture directly on to the bird table. Simple! By the way, don't be tempted to give the birds margarine or low-fat spreads because these can interfere with the insulating qualities of their feathers if they come into contact with them.

✎ Rice is nice ✎

Rice is an excellent bird food in the winter, but you must ensure it's cooked. If it's raw, it will swell up inside the birds' guts and could kill them. Conversely, you should never put out cooked porridge in case it forms a hard shell around the birds' beaks. Give them uncooked oats with a supply of clean water nearby.

✎ Spuds-they-like ✎

Cooked potatoes are a good source of food for birds, so instead of wolfing down those leftover roast potatoes when no one is looking, perhaps you could do your waistline a favour and donate them to the birds instead. They don't much care for chips, but will happily dine on potatoes that have been mashed, boiled, baked or roasted.

✎ Touts des fruits ✎

If you've ever watched birds stripping your prize cherry tree, you'll know that they like fruit. Soak dried fruits, such as raisins and sultanas, in water before putting them out in the spring and summer.

Instead of throwing away apples or pears that have gone soft, cut them up and give them to the birds. If you're really British and have an abundant apple or pear tree, you could freeze plenty of the windfalls and put out a few of them at a time, defrosted and cut up, during the winter months.

✎ Tasty pastry ✎

Next time you roll out some pastry and you're left with the offcuts, consider donating them to the birds. They won't mind if you cook the pastry first or give it to them raw. Cheesy pastry will make them extra happy.

✎ Pet food ✎

In the summer, birds enjoy meaty cat and dog food. It's a good substitute for the earthworms that they normally eat but which are often scarce in the summer months. Dog biscuits soaked in water are also a good food for birds in the summer. However, you must watch to ensure that the food doesn't attract lots of local moggies that will then be delighted to add the birds you're trying to feed to their own diets.

✎ And finally . . . ✎

Here are some foods that you should never give to birds.

Steer clear of anything that's gone mouldy as it won't do them any good at all. They can't metabolise salt, so avoid giving them salty bacon, ham, pepperoni, salami or anything else that's been cured with salt. Don't give them salted nuts, either. Unsalted nuts are an excellent bird food, but don't put out large chunks or whole nuts in the spring, summer or autumn, as these could choke fledglings and small birds. Peanuts are another good food, but they can sometimes be contaminated by a toxin that kills birds, so buy them from a reputable company or look on the packet for an assurance that they are free from aflatoxin. Although you can give them small amounts of white bread, you should provide plenty of other food as well to boost their nutritional uptake. Always soak large pieces of bread to avoid small birds choking on it. Seed mixtures can be very good, but don't buy any that contain dried pulses, such as lentils, because these will swell up inside the birds' guts and could kill them. Desiccated coconut is another food that could kill birds for the same reason, although they will enjoy pecking at half a shell of fresh coconut if you hang it from a tree or bird table.

SWANNING AROUND

There's no mistaking a swan. With its white feathers (in the northern hemisphere; southern hemisphere swans are black and white), serpentine neck and colourful beak, the swan is one of the most distinctive members of the bird kingdom. It also has lots of legends and stories associated with it. But how many of them are true? And how many different species of swan are there in Britain?

The one and only

Although three types of swan can be seen in Britain, there is only one native species. This is the mute swan (*Cygnus olor*). In common with the other swans that only visit Britain, the mute swan has beautiful white feathers. It's easily identified by its long orange bill with a black base. You can see the mute swan in most of the United Kingdom, although you won't find it in parts of northern Scotland and mid Wales. It eats snails, insects and aquatic plants. Although it's called mute, it does have a voice, but admittedly it's quieter than other swans.

≈ Royal swans ≈

It's often said that the reigning monarch is the legal owner of every swan in Britain, but is this really true? Up to a point, yes. For a start, this assumed royal ownership applies solely to the mute swan (*Cygnus olor*), and not to the two species of summer visitor. But why did the Crown want to own all the swans in the first place?

GRUB UP

In medieval Britain, swans were considered to be the perfect food to serve up at banquets and feasts. (No wonder swans can be so unfriendly towards humans. Quite understandably, they don't want to end up in someone's oven surrounded by roast potatoes.) Rather than risk these apparently delicious creatures being captured and cooked by ordinary people, in the 12th century the Crown decided to assume ownership of any privately owned swan that escaped from its natural confines. The next step was to announce that all swans owned by people who paid less than five marks in rent each year were now forfeit to the Crown. A Keeper of the King's Swans was appointed to ensure that the system worked properly.

SWAN UPPING

In the 15th century, royal ownership of wild swans began to be shared with the Worshipful Company of Vintners and the Worshipful Company of Dyers, which are two of the livery companies of the City of London. Rather than have lots of swans wandering around with no one knowing who they belonged to, each swan had to be given some

easily recognisable identification. The process of checking this identification, and conferring it on cygnets (baby swans), was carried out
during the third week of each July in a special ceremony called Swan
Upping. Royal swans were left unmarked (and still are), but those
belonging to the Dyers' Company were given a nick on one side of
their beaks (today, they are ringed on one leg), and those belonging
to the Vintners' Company were marked on either side of their beaks
(now they are ringed on each leg).

The Crown now only exercises its ownership on the swans living
along certain stretches of the River Thames and its tributaries, even
though technically it owns all unmarked swans living in open water in
Britain. Swan Upping still continues, led by the Queen's Swan Marker
and conducted by the Swan Uppers, although it now has a scientific
focus because it's an annual census of the swans living on the Thames,
and it also checks them for damage caused by fishing lines and other
hazards.

❧ Visiting swans ❧

Although mute swans are the only native British swan, each year they
are joined by two visiting breeds. The whooper swan (*Cygnus cygnus*)
spends each spring and summer in Iceland before flying into Britain
in October and staying for six months. It's smaller than the mute
swan, and its beak has a large yellow triangle. You can see this swan
in Northern Ireland, plus parts of Scotland, northern England and
East Anglia. The Bewick's swan (*Cygnus columbianus*) flies in from
Siberia in the middle of October and stays until the following March.
You can see it in parts of Northern Ireland, Wales and southern
England. It's the smallest of the three swans to be found in Britain,
and looks rather like a goose. The black area on its bill is larger than
that of the mute and whooper swans.

❧ Do swans really mate for life? ❧

Although swans don't always stay with a partner for life (even
swans can recognise the necessity for a divorce sometimes) they are

monogamous. They like to live in the same place, and will return to the same nesting site year after year. The old nest isn't wasted, because they either reuse it or rebuild it. They create this nest – which is a large, rather untidy-looking affair made from straw, reeds, sticks and other organic material – on a mound situated on the edge of a stretch of water, such as a river or lake.

Preparation for the arrival of the cygnets is a fair division of labour for mute swans, with the cob (male) fetching the nesting materials and the pen (female) fashioning them into a nest. After the pen has laid her clutch of up to seven eggs in late April to early May, she and the cob take it in turns to incubate them. When the cygnets have hatched (a process that takes between 35 and 41 days), the cob and pen once again share all the family duties. They both take care of the cygnets, and both take them out on the water, but the cob is particularly protective of them and will noisily see off any potential threats with some very aggressive behaviour. It takes six months for cygnets to learn to fly, and their parents are always vigilant in their defence during this time. At this stage, cygnets have black beaks and grey, fluffy plumage, so they look very different from their elegant parents. Some pairs of swans will send their cygnets on their way as soon as their plumage begins to turn white in the autumn, whereas others will take their cygnets with them when they go off to join a large flock of overwintering swans. These cygnets stay with the flock in the following spring, while their parents return to their nesting site to raise a new family.

➣ Do swans really have swansongs? ➣

There is a legend that mute swans are completely silent throughout their lives and then sing a beautiful song before they die. However, this is simply a nice story because the opposite is true: mute swans aren't mute, and neither do they burst into song shortly before death.

WISE OLD OWLS

Owls are among the most revered birds in Britain. Whether it's their relative scarcity value, the fact that you can normally only see them at dusk or dawn, their beautiful appearance or their enigmatic aura, they're always a source of great interest. Five breeds of owl live in Britain, but some are more rare than others. Changes in the way the countryside has been farmed for the past seventy years, with the emphasis on intensive farming rather than continuing to sustain natural habitats for wildlife, has meant that what were once rich hunting grounds are now in great decline for owls.

∾ Barn owl (*Tyto alba*) ∾

This is the species that normally springs to mind when owls are mentioned. The barn owl is very distinctive, thanks to its black eyes, heart-shaped face surrounded by a ruff of buff feathers, and its white chest, tummy and the undersides of its wings. Its call is a screech and because it's nocturnal it's most commonly seen at dusk and dawn. Barn owls hunt for food along the unkempt edges of fields, woods and stretches of water, and their favourite foods are voles and other rodents. This means that if you want the chance of seeing barn owls in your own garden, you must provide plenty of rough grass for them to hunt through, as well as perching posts along stretches of fence. Barn owls are distributed throughout England, Wales and Northern Ireland, as well as parts of Scotland.

✎ Little owl (*Athene noctua*) ✎

This owl was introduced to Britain in the 19th century and is now a naturalised inhabitant of England and Wales. A small owl, as its name implies, it has brown and cream speckled feathers, long legs and characteristic white feathers above its eyes that look like eyebrows. Its head bobs up and down when it's alarmed. The little owl can often be seen perching on branches or telegraph poles during the day, and can become quite used to the human activity that may be going on around it. Its call is a piercing 'kee-ou'. It eats worms, insects, and small mammals and birds, which it chases with a bounding flight.

✎ Long-eared owl (*Asio otus*) ✎

Although its name suggests that this owl has long ears, in fact it has long ear tufts on top of its head that make it very easy to identify. Its call is a hollow 'whoo'. Sadly, there aren't many breeding pairs in Britain, and it's almost completely absent from southern and southwest England, and also south Wales. The long-eared owls that do live in Britain are very elusive and nocturnal, so the chances of seeing them in the wild are fairly rare unless you spot some birds that are migrating from other countries. The long-eared owl eats small rodents, and tops up its diet with small birds in winter.

✎ Short-eared owl (*Asio flammeus*) ✎

Another owl with a heart-shaped face, the short-eared owl has yellow eyes, buff feathers on its face and underparts, and pale feathers on the undersides of its wings. These are tipped with black, and it has a distinctive flight in which the wings flap deeply up and down before settling into a shallow V-shape as it glides. Its call is a whooping sound, and its prey is small mammals, including voles. Although some short-eared owls live permanently in Britain, many fly in for the winter from Scandinavia, Iceland and Russia, so there is more chance of seeing them at this time of year. They can be seen, at varying times of the year, throughout England, Wales and Scotland, as well as parts of Northern Ireland.

⇌ Tawny owl (*Strix aluco*) ⇌

The tawny owl has a characteristic widow's peak of dark feathers on the top of its round head, mottled brown feathers on its disc-shaped face and squat body, and huge black eyes. It's a nocturnal creature and you're far more likely to hear its characteristic, breathy 'whoo-whoo-whoo' call than to see the bird itself. (When you hear the classic 'tuwhit-tuwhoo' call of the tawny owl, it's actually a pair calling to one another, with the female calling 'kee-wick' and the male responding with 'whoo'.) Sometimes, you may see the tawny owl swooping down on small birds, especially if they're dining at your bird table, and carrying them off. It also eats small rodents, small mammals, frogs and worms. Once they form breeding pairs, tawny owls rarely leave their breeding grounds. You will find them all year round throughout England, Wales and Scotland, but not in Northern Ireland.

COMMON BRITISH BIRDS

Many different birds fly in and out of Britain according to the season, while others stay put throughout the year. Here is a selection of some of the birds you may be lucky enough to see.

⇌ Summer visitors ⇌

Common sandpiper (*Actitis hypoleucos*)
Cuckoo (*Cuculus canorus*)
Dotterel (*Charadrius morinellus*)

Garden warbler (*Sylvia borin*)
Grasshopper warbler (*Locustella naevia*)
House martin (*Delichon urbica*)
Lesser whitethroat (*Sylvia curruca*)
Nightjar (*Caprimulgus europaeus*)
Osprey (*Pandion haliaetus*)
Pied flycatcher (*Ficedula hypoleuca*)
Quail (*Coturnix coturnix*)
Ring ouzel (*Turdus torquatus*)
Sand martin (*Riparia riparia*)
Spotted flycatcher (*Muscicapa striata*)

Swallow (*Hirundo rustica*)
Swift (*Apus apus*)
Tree pipit (*Anthus trivialis*)
Wheatear (*Oenanthe oenanthe*)
Whimbrel (*Numenius phaeopus*)
Whinchat (*Saxicola rubetra*)
Whitethroat (*Sylvia communis*)
Willow warbler (*Phylloscopus trochilus*)
Wood warbler (*Phylloscopus sibilatrix*)
Yellow wagtail (*Motacilla flava*)

❧ Winter visitors ❧

Bewick's swan (*Cygnus columbianus*)
Brambling (*Fringilla montifringilla*)
Fieldfare (*Turdus pilaris*)
Great grey shrike (*Lanius excubitor*)
Jack snipe (*Lymnocryptes minimus*)
Pink-footed goose (*Anser brachyrhynchus*)
Shorelark (*Eremophila alpestris*)
Waxwing (*Bombycilla garrulus*)
White-fronted goose (*Anser albifrons*)
Whooper swan (*Cygnus cygnus*)

❧ Birds seen in Britain all year round ❧

Barn owl (*Tyto alba*)
Blackbird (*Turdus merula*)
Blackcap (*Sylvia atricapilla*)
Black-headed gull (*Larus ridibundus*)
Black-tailed godwit (*Limosa limosa*)
Blue tit (*Cyanistes caeruleus*)
Bullfinch (*Pyrrhula pyrrhula*)
Buzzard (*Buteo buteo*)
Canada goose (*Branta canadensis*)
Carrion crow (*Corvus corone*)
Chaffinch (*Fringilla coelebs*)
Chiffchaff (*Phylloscopus collybita*)
Coal tit (*Periparus ater*)
Collared dove (*Streptopelia decaocto*)
Common gull (*Larus canus*)
Common tern (*Sterna hirundo*)
Coot (*Fulica atra*)

Corn bunting (*Miliaria calandra*)
Crossbill (*Loxia curvirostra*)
Curlew (*Numenius arquata*)
Dipper (*Cinclus cinclus*)
Dunnock (*Prunella modularis*)
Goldcrest (*Regulus regulus*)
Goldeneye (*Bucephala clangula*)
Golden plover (*Pluvialis apricaria*)
Goldfinch (*Carduelis carduelis*)
Great black-backed gull (*Larus marinus*)
Great spotted woodpecker (*Dendrocopos major*)
Great tit (*Parus major*)
Greenfinch (*Carduelis chloris*)
Green sandpiper (*Tringa ochropus*)
Greenshank (*Tringa nebularia*)
Green woodpecker (*Picus viridis*)
Grey heron (*Ardea cinerea*)
Greylag goose (*Anser anser*)
Grey partridge (*Perdix perdix*)
Grey wagtail (*Motacilla cinerea*)
Hawfinch (*Coccothraustes coccothraustes*)
Hen harrier (*Circus cyaneus*)
Herring gull (*Larus argentatus*)
House sparrow (*Passer domesticus*)
Jackdaw (*Corvus monedula*)
Jay (*Garrulus glandarius*)
Kestrel (*Falco tinnunculus*)
Kingfisher (*Alcedo atthis*)
Lapwing (*Vanellus vanellus*)
Lesser black-backed gull (*Larus fuscus*)
Linnet (*Carduelis cannabina*)
Little grebe (*Tachybaptus ruficollis*)

Little owl (*Athene noctua*)
Long-eared owl (*Asio otus*)
Long-tailed tit (*Aegithalos caudatus*)
Magpie (*Pica pica*)
Mallard (*Anas platyrhynchos*)
Meadow pipit (*Anthus pratensis*)
Merlin (*Falco columbarius*)
Mistle thrush (*Turdus viscivorus*)
Moorhen (*Gallinula chloropus*)
Mute swan (*Cygnus olor*)

Nuthatch (*Sitta europaea*)
Oystercatcher (*Haematopus ostralegus*)
Peregrine (*Falco peregrinus*)
Pheasant (*Phasianus colchicus*)
Pied wagtail (*Motacilla alba*)
Pochard (*Aythya ferina*)
Raven (*Corvus corax*)
Red-legged partridge (*Alectoris rufa*)
Redpoll (*Carduelis flammea*)
Redshank (*Tringa totanus*)
Redstart (*Phoenicurus phoenicurus*)
Redwing (*Turdus iliacus*)

Reed bunting (*Emberiza schoeniclus*)

Ringed plover (*Charadrius hiaticula*)

Robin (*Erithacus rubecula*)

Rook (*Corvus frugilegus*)

Ruff (*Philomachus pugnax*)

Sedge warbler (*Acrocephalus schoenobaenus*)

Short-eared owl (*Asio flammeus*)

Shoveler (*Anas clypeata*)

Siskin (*Carduelis spinus*)

Skylark (*Alauda arvensis*)

Snipe (*Gallinago gallinago*)

Snow bunting (*Plectrophenax nivalis*)

Song thrush (*Turdus philomelos*)

Sparrowhawk (*Accipiter nisus*)

Spotted redshank (*Tringa erythropus*)

Starling (*Sturnus vulgaris*)

Stonechat (*Saxicola torquata*)

Tawny owl (*Strix aluco*)

Teal (*Anas crecca*)

Treecreeper (*Certhia familiaris*)

Tree sparrow (*Passer montanus*)

Tufted duck (*Aythya fuligula*)

Water rail (*Rallus aquaticus*)

Widgeon (*Anas penelope*)

Willow grouse (*Lagopus lagopus*)

Woodcock (*Scolopax rusticola*)

Woodpigeon (*Columba palumbus*)

Wood sandpiper (*Tringa glareola*)

Wren (*Troglodytes troglodytes*)

Yellowhammer (*Emberiza citrinella*)

THE GREAT OUTDOORS

Of all the trees that grow so fair,
Old England to adorn,
Greater are none beneath the Sun
Than Oak, and Ash, and Thorn.

'A TREE SONG', RUDYARD KIPLING

BRITAIN'S NATIVE TREES

Many different species of trees grow in Britain, but only thirty-three of them are native. This means that they were established in what are now the British Isles after the end of the last Ice Age (roughly twenty thousand years ago) and before the rising sea levels turned the land mass into islands separated from the rest of Europe.

Aspen (*Populus tremula*)
Bay willow (*Salix pentandra*)
Beech (*Fagus sylvatica*)
Bird cherry (*Prunus padus*)
Black poplar (*Populus nigra* var. *betulifolia*)
Box (*Buxus sempervirens*)
Broad-leafed lime (*Tilia platyphyllos*)
Common alder (*Alnus glutinosa*)
Common ash (*Fraxinus excelsior*)
Common juniper (*Juniperus communis*)
Common oak (*Quercus robur*)
Crab apple (*Malus sylvestris*)

Crack willow (*Salix fragilis*)

Downy birch (*Betula pubescens*)

Field maple (*Acer campestre*)

Goat willow (*Salix caprea*)

Hawthorn (*Crataegus monogyna*)

Hazel (*Corylus avellana*)

Holly (*Ilex aquifolium*)

Hornbeam (*Carpinus betulus*)

Midland hawthorn (*Crataegus laevigata*)

Rowan (*Sorbus aucuparia*)

Scots pine (*Pinus sylvestris*)

Sessile oak (*Quercus petraea*)

Silver birch (*Betula pendula*)

Small-leafed lime (*Tilia cordata*)

Strawberry tree (*Arbutus unedo*)

Whitebeam (*Sorbus aria*)

White willow (*Salix alba*)

Wild cherry (*Prunus avium*)

Wild service tree (*Sorbus torminalis*)

Wych elm (*Ulmus glabra*)

Yew (*Taxus baccata*)

HOW TO TELL THE AGE OF AN OAK TREE

There are two methods for doing this, and they're neatly divided into the simple and the complicated.

Taking the simple one first (although it's not as accurate as the complicated method), all you need is a measuring tape. Using centimetres, measure the circumference of the trunk at the point where it is 1.5m from the ground. Divide this number by 2.5, and the result is the age of the tree. However, this is only a rough estimate because trees put on different amounts of growth according to their living conditions.

The complicated method is much more exact, but not necessarily convenient or easy because you use a boring bar to remove a core of wood from the trunk of the tree. When you examine the plug of wood you'll be able to count the rings, which will give you the age of the tree. That's because the tree puts on a layer of growth each year, at the point between the previous year's growth of wood and the bark. The better the growing season, the wider this layer will be. Each layer consists of two colours of wood: the light layer is the wood put on in the spring and summer, and the dark layer is the wood put on in the autumn and winter.

If the tree has been felled and the trunk cut in half, you can count the number of concentric rings that are visible.

LIGHTING A FIRE WITHOUT MATCHES

Don't despair if you ever need to light a fire but don't have any matches to hand. You don't need them, although you do need something with which to strike a spark. You also need a decent penknife or Swiss Army knife. Here's what to do.

First of all, make a little bundle of tinder, such as shavings of dry wood, very dry grass or patches of the bark from birch trees. You'll need this to hand as soon as you've made some sparks.

Here comes the difficult part, because it involves producing the initial spark that will become the fire, and this can be hard work. One classic method is to create a spark from the friction that's produced when two pieces of wood are rubbed against each other. Find a flat, dry piece of softwood, such as willow or juniper, a long stick that will act as a spindle, and a flat segment of dry birch bark. Make a small hollow in the flat piece of softwood and cut a V-shaped notch next to it, on the edge of the wood. Place the flat piece of wood on the ground, with the segment of bark positioned beneath the notch. Put one end of the long spindle in the hollow and start rolling it back and forth, as fast as you can, between the palms of your hands. When the tip of the spindle starts to glow, you tap the flat piece of wood so the ember drops on to the bark. Now carefully transfer it to the bundle of tinder and start to blow on it to fan that spark into a flame. You can use this to light a fire.

THE CLEAN AIR ACT

Want to know if the air around your home is clean? Go outside and look for lichens, because they don't grow in areas of heavy pollution.

Lichens are tiny organisms that are a combination of fungus and algae. The fungus is the main component, but the algae are essential for the lichens to photosynthesise and therefore obtain food from the atmosphere. You'll find them on the bark of trees, on fences, on the branches of hedges, on pots and other containers, on railings, on stones, on roof tiles, on wooden benches and pretty much anywhere else that takes their fancy. Have a good look around and see if you can spot different species. If you can't see any lichen at all, it means you live in an area where the air is badly polluted.

❧ The different types of lichen ❧

There are four types of lichen, each of which is a reliable indicator of the particular quality of the surrounding air. So if you can become acquainted with some of the different species you will discover the cleanliness – or otherwise – of the air around your home. If the air is polluted, you will find crustose lichen (these look crusty and can only be removed from the bark of trees by cutting the bark). If the air is moderately clean, you'll find squamulose (scale-like) lichen. If the air is clean, you'll see foliose (leaf-like) and fruticose (shrub-like) lichen. And if the air is really clean, you'll find a few species that will only thrive in those conditions.

It pays to learn a little about lichen because, as the air gets cleaner, some species are staging a comeback. For instance, some types of lichens are now being seen in London for the first time in two hundred years.

While you're about it, have a look for moss growing on roofs. It's been proliferating in recent years, thanks to the improvement in air quality. Like lichen, moss won't grow where the air is very polluted.

Looking for moss, and precisely identifying the lichens that grow in your neighbourhood, will give you interesting insights into the air you're breathing.

STAYING WARM IN THE SNOW

It's not only children who love to rush out into the snow the moment they spot the first flake. Lots of adults enjoy it, too. But how can you stay warm while you're busy building snowmen and having snowball fights?

❧ Traditional methods ❧

In the past, people had various ways of keeping warm in cold weather. One classic method, which wouldn't endear you to your friends and family if you tried it now, was to put on several layers of flannel underwear in the autumn and not remove them again until the advent of warmer weather in the late spring. It's sometimes been claimed that children were sewn into their underclothes each autumn so there was no danger of them falling off.

On the whole, our ancestors were much more active than we are today, so they also kept warm by keeping on the move. They didn't have time to huddle over their fires because they were too busy getting through all the chores without the aid of the labour-saving devices we tend to take for granted now. If they were outside in snowy weather, they were more likely to be chopping wood, getting in the chickens or walking to market to buy food than to be throwing snowballs at each other.

If they were really brave, or it was extremely cold, some people would smear goose fat on their bodies before covering themselves in their flannel underwear. Of course, this would only have added to the stink but presumably everyone got used to that because it was so prevalent.

❧ Wear your thermals! ❧

Sensible underwear (even if you don't take it off all winter) has long been one of the best ways of keeping warm. Our male ancestors wore long johns and long-sleeved vests, and our female ancestors wore long-legged knickers (or 'drawers', as they were often called) and bodices. So before you start thinking about what else you should wear, you must put on your thermals. Yes, skimpy underwear may be a lot more attractive, but that isn't the point. Ideally, you should put on some thermal long johns and a long-sleeved thermal vest. If you don't have any long johns, wear some thick tights.

❧ The insulating layers ❧

Our forefathers always piled on the layers of clothing because they knew that these trap warm air to insulate them from the cold. It's still much more effective to wear several thin layers of clothing than one thick item. Also, if you work up a sweat while outside you can remove one of the layers without freezing. Wool is a good choice. When choosing your trousers, corduroy or moleskin is better than denim, which can quickly make you cold.

❧ Keep your core warm ❧

It's essential that you keep the core of your body warm, so make sure your trunk is well covered up. This will help to keep potential ailments at bay, such as a chill or nagging backache. Choose clothes that overlap, such as a long-sleeved T-shirt that will tuck into your trousers. The last thing you want is gaps where the cold can strike.

❧ The outer shell ❧

The outdoor clothes you wear on top of your ordinary clothes should form a protective shell between you and the elements. So wear a waterproof jacket, preferably with an insulated lining. Never mind if it makes you look like the Michelin Man – this isn't a fashion parade. And put on some thick, waterproof boots, too, ideally with a warm lining. Wellington boots are OK for a short time but your feet will soon start to get very cold, which could lead to cramp. Make sure, too, that your boots have non-slip soles to reduce your chances of falling over. If you have ski boots, these would be perfect for having fun in the garden or going on a snowy walk.

❧ Don't forget your extremities ❧

Put on one pair of cotton socks followed by a pair of woollen socks so you stand a good chance of keeping your feet warm. Make sure they're long socks, not dainty little things that stop at your ankles.

Our female ancestors wore long woollen stockings and helped to cover up the gap at the tops of their legs with several flannel petticoats. The men wore long woollen socks held up with suspenders.

In the past, most people wore mittens or fingerless gloves in the winter, to avoid the misery that comes from having cold wrists and hands. You must wear gloves, too, when you're outdoors and ideally they should be waterproof to avoid getting soggy fingers (they'll be agony when they start warming up again). If you don't have such things as waterproof gloves, wear ordinary household rubber gloves over a pair of woollen or fleece gloves. Put on a hat or wrap your head in a thick scarf. And make sure you've got a scarf round your neck, too, otherwise your neck muscles could tense up in the cold. Both men and women used to swathe their necks and shoulders in several woollen shawls and scarves.

≈ Take reinforcements ≈

In the past, people understood only too well the importance of eating and drinking something hot in order to keep warm. If you're planning to spend a long time outdoors – or even a short time, if it's very cold – it's a good idea to take a vacuum flask of a hot drink or soup with you. This will soon warm you up if you get chilled. Before you go out, though, it's a good idea to eat something hot, so not only does your body have some fuel on which to draw but your tummy feels warm, too.

≈ Be sensible ≈

You'll soon get cold if you stand or sit in one place for too long, so keep on the move.

Put some moisturising cream on your face to stop the skin getting too dry, and protect your lips with a lip salve. If it's a sunny day, the glare from the snow could give you sunburn, so consider putting on some sun cream.

If you're out walking and you get caught in a blizzard, seek shelter as soon as possible, especially if the wind is strong, otherwise you'll become very chilled very quickly. Take your mobile phone with you in case you need to ring for help.

Watch out for signs of frostbite, which occurs when the tissues in your body become so cold that nerve damage occurs. This is a serious condition that needs urgent medical attention.

Finally, go indoors to warm up before you start to get really cold. You can always venture out again once you've thawed out.

A-FORAGING WE WILL GO

Nature has provided us with a rich larder of wild foods that we can eat, if we only know what we're looking for. These foods are delicious, nutritious and free. However, it's only sensible to be cautious, so you must be certain that what you're picking is edible and safe, and also that it isn't someone else's property. Picking blackberries and sloes in a country lane bordered on both sides by fields is one thing, but helping yourself to the bounty in the hedges that enclose someone's house is quite another. You should avoid picking food that grows beside busy roads, as it will probably have absorbed the exhaust fumes from cars. Here are some of the countryside foods that are often sought by foragers.

≈ Blackberries (*Rubus fruticosus*) ≈

Blackberries are abundant each autumn, but you'll find that some plants have fatter and juicier berries than others. These are the ones to go for. The hefty thorns on the blackberry cables mean you should expect to be scratched and pricked, and your clothes may also become stained by blackberry juice if you aren't careful. Blackberries appear earlier in some years than in others, depending on the warmth of the summer. Folklore states that you should never pick blackberries after Michaelmas (29 September) because that's when the Devil spits on them. Whether or not you believe in the Devil it's a wise precaution because blackberries can get very flyblown and mildewy after this date.

≈ Elderberries (*Sambucus nigra*) ≈

The elder bush provides two offerings each year. Its first gift is the foamy, cream flowers that appear in summer and which make the most delicious elderflower cordial if you boil them with water and sugar. They also make a lovely wine (see pages 261–3). Leave some on the bush, though, so they can turn into beautiful purple elderberries in the autumn. These make a wonderful country wine, too. However, don't strip the bush of all the berries because they're an important food for birds.

≈ Mushrooms ≈

Autumn is the time of year for wild mushrooms, which can spring up in fields and woods with all the fecundity of . . . well, mushrooms. Depending on where you look, you can find a rich selection of edible mushrooms, such as field mushrooms (*Agaricus campestris*), ceps (*Boletus edulis*), chanterelles (*Cantharellus cibarius*) and oyster mushrooms (*Pleurotus ostreatus*), but it's absolutely essential that you know what you're looking for and what to avoid. Each autumn there are terrible news stories about people who thought they were picking and eating edible mushrooms that turned out to be poisonous, sometimes with fatal results. The theory that poisonous mushrooms always look unpleasant or have a nasty smell is a complete fallacy, akin to the idea that mass-murderers always have horns on their heads. If you've never picked wild mushrooms before, don't touch anything that hasn't been verified by an expert. And invest in a good book on mushrooms, so you begin to learn what you're looking at and can discover how to tell edible mushrooms from their toxic look-alikes. Never, ever, take a chance and hope for the best.

≈ Sloes (*Prunus spinosa*) ≈

These small, hard, purple berries are borne by the blackthorn each autumn, and you can find them in great abundance in hedgerows. Be careful when picking them because the blackthorn has long, vicious thorns that can cause blood poisoning if you're very unlucky. The sloes are far too hard and bitter to eat raw but they make fabulous sloe gin (see page 196–7).

≈ Stinging nettles (*Urtica dioica*) ≈

It may seem a crazy idea if your only experience of stinging nettles is a nasty brush with them that leaves you feeling as though your skin is being pierced by red-hot needles, but stinging nettles are extremely good to eat. They're also good for you, with high levels of vitamins A, C, D and K, plus calcium, iron, potassium and manganese. As with all wild foods, though, you have to pick your moment. You must also wear gloves, for obvious reasons.

Always pick stinging needles when the plants are young, and then only take the top two leaves from each plant because these are the most succulent. Never pick leaves from a plant that's in flower or setting seed because they will contain a urinary irritant. Folklore states that nettle leaves should be picked before May Day (1 May) because after that the Devil uses the leaves to make his shirts.

Never eat stinging nettles raw because your mouth and throat will be covered in painful stings. After cooking the leaves you can eat them like spinach, or you can make a delicious soup from them. You can also make nettle tea by putting some fresh leaves in a teapot and steeping them in boiling water.

⮞ Weeds ⮜

It's often been said by gardeners that a weed is merely a plant that's growing in the wrong place. As far as foragers are concerned, a weed is often a plant that can be eaten. You may be surprised to know that some of the following weeds are edible. If you have a garden, it's good to know that you can get your own back on some of these abundant weeds by turning them into lunch.

The young leaves of the tall, clinging weed commonly known as goose grass or cleavers (*Galium aparine*) are good in salads. So are the young leaves of Jack-by-the-hedge (*Alliaria petiolata*) and hawthorn (*Crataegus monogyna*). The leaves of young dandelions (*Taraxacum officinale*) give a delicious bitter touch to salads and are high in vitamin A and potassium. Wild garlic (*Allium ursinum*) grows plentifully and has a milder flavour than its cultivated cousin; you can eat the bulbs, leaves and flowers. However, the leaves resemble various poisonous plants, so make sure you know what you're picking. When you rub the leaves between your fingers you should be able to smell their characteristic garlicky odour. If you can't, don't pick them.

Up the Garden Path

Here's flowers for you;
Hot lavender, mints, savory, marjoram;
The marigold that goes to bed wi' the sun,
And with him rises weeping.

THE WINTER'S TALE, WILLIAM SHAKESPEARE

A BEE-FILLED GARDEN

These busy creatures pollinate many of the plants we eat, yet some species are in serious decline for reasons that have yet to be discovered. We need to create favourable environments for them, especially in our own gardens.

Bees feed on the nectar of plants, so if you want to invite bees into your garden you must provide them with plenty of food. Here are some of the plants that bees most enjoy. Together, they will cater for honey-bees as well as bumble bees, solitary bees and mason bees. As a bonus, many of the plants also appeal to butterflies and moths, to bring your garden truly alive.

❧ Suitable spring plants ❧

Californian lilac (*Ceanothus divergens*)
Candelabra primula (*Primula chungensis*)
Cherry laurel (*Prunus laurocerasus*)
Crab apple (*Malus sylvestris*)
Daisy (*Bellis perennis*)
English bluebell (*Hyacinthoides non-scripta*)
Marsh marigold (*Caltha palustris*)
Spindle (*Euonymus europaeus*)

❧ Suitable summer plants ❧

Barberry (*Berberis* x *stenophylla*)
Basil thyme (*Clinopodium acinos*)

Bergamot (*Monarda didyma*)
Californian poppy (*Eschscholzia californica*)
Catmint (*Nepeta* x *faassenii*)
Daisy (*Bellis perennis*)
Dill (*Anethum graveolens*)
Feverfew (*Tanacetum parthenium*)
Hedgerow cranesbill (*Geranium pyrenaicum*)
Jacob's ladder (*Polemonium caeruleum*)
Wormwood (*Artemisia absinthum*)

❧ Suitable autumn plants ❧

Autumn hawkbit (*Leontodon autumnalis*)
Black-eyed Susan (*Rudbeckia hirta*)
Borage (*Borago officinalis*)
Clarkia sp.
Cosmos (*Cosmos atrosanguineus*)
Daisy (*Bellis perennis*)
Pennyroyal (*Mentha pulegium*)
Red valerian (*Centranthus ruber*)
Strawberry clover (*Trifolium fragiferum*)

HOW TO ATTRACT BUTTERFLIES AND MOTHS INTO YOUR GARDEN

Our gardens wouldn't be the same without the activities of the many butterflies and moths that visit them each year, yet some varieties that were once common are now becoming endangered. Increasingly intensive farming practices, plus the widespread use of agricultural weedkillers and the frequent grubbing up of ancient hedges, means that these days butterflies and moths need all the help they can get. If you have a garden, planting a year-round succession of flowers and shrubs that provide the nectar needed by these creatures will help to ensure their continued survival. Whenever possible, choose open-pollinated plants rather than hybrids, and single rather than double flowers as these contain more nectar.

Do your best to site the nectar plants in the warm, sheltered and sunny spots that butterflies and moths love. Arrange each variety of plants in a block, so there are plenty of flowers to go round. Avoid putting any garden chemicals on or near these plants, otherwise you'll kill the very insects you are trying to attract. Better still, start gardening organically. Keep the plants dead-headed and well watered to ensure a prolonged display. More flowers mean more food for these insects. At the end of the flowering season, some flower seeds provide valuable food for birds so it makes sense to leave the dead flowerheads on the plants. These have the added benefit of looking very architectural on frosty mornings.

If possible, grow some wildflowers too and leave at least one corner of your garden a little untidy, with some stinging nettles, brambles, heaps of dead leaves and log piles in which caterpillars can overwinter. A few weeds in the lawn will add to the range of foodplants on offer.

≈ Suitable spring plants ≈

Arabis sp.

Aubrieta sp.

Common dog-violet (*Viola riviniana*)

Cowslip (*Primula veris*)

Dandelion (*Taraxacum officinale*)

English bluebell (*Hyacinthoides non-scripta*)

Forget-me-not (*Myosotis* sp.)

Honesty (*Lunaria* sp.)

Lady's smock (*Cardamine pratensis*)

Lilac (*Syringa* sp.)
Lungwort (*Pulmonaria* sp.)
Pansy (*Viola* sp.)
Rosemary (*Rosmarinus* sp.)
Skimmia sp.
Wallflowers (*Erysimum* sp.)

❧ Suitable summer plants ❧

Buddleia (*Buddleja* sp.)
Catmint (*Nepeta* sp.)
Chives (*Allium schoenoprasum*)
Common bird's-foot trefoil (*Lotus corniculatus*)
Cornflower (*Centaurea cyanus*)
Greater bird's-foot trefoil (*Lotus pedunculatus*)
Hardy geranium (*Geranium* sp.)
Hebe sp.
Holly (*Ilex* sp.)
Honeysuckle (*Lonicera* sp.)
Horseshoe vetch (*Hippocrepis comosa*)
Jasmine (*Jasminum officinale*)
Lavender (*Lavandula* sp.)
Marjoram (*Origanum* sp.)
Mint (*Mentha* sp.)
Nasturtium (*Tropaeolum* sp.)
Purple loosestrife (*Lythrum salicaria*)
Red valerian (*Centranthus rubra*)

Scabious (*Scabiosa*)

Thyme (*Thymus*)

⮞ Suitable autumn plants ⮜

Chrysanthemum sp.

Evening primrose (*Oenothera* sp.)

Ice plant (*Sedum spectabile*)

Ivy (*Hedera helix*)

Michaelmas daisy (*Aster novi-belgii*)

Night-scented stock (*Matthiola longipetala*)

Tobacco plant (*Nicotiana sylvestris*)

BUILDING THE PERFECT BONFIRE

Oh, the joys of a bonfire. Such things may be frowned upon in towns and cities because of the smoke they create, but they are still prevalent in the countryside. Besides, the ash that's left when the bonfire has cooled down contains potash, which is just what flowers and fruiting plants need to ensure a good crop. But first, you need to know how to light the perfect bonfire.

Choose a fine day, preferably with a light breeze rather than a howling gale. If you have neighbours and you want to stay friendly with them, you must opt for a day when the wind isn't blowing in their direction. If you're surrounded by neighbours, wait for a day when there is almost no wind so the smoke can rise straight into the air. It might be a wise precaution to check the weather forecast, too, to ensure that the wind isn't about to pick up.

Many people have a special patch of garden for their bonfire. It's common sense to choose a clear area that isn't overhung by trees, because you don't want to scorch or set light to them. Watch out for nearby hedges, shrubs or flowers, for the same reason. Check the ground to make sure it's clear of roots, because accidentally setting light to these may mean the fire spreads underground, and that could be disastrous.

✎ Preparing the fire ✎

Now find the wood you'll be burning and divide it into three sizes: kindling, to get the fire going; slightly larger twigs to feed it; and finally logs or big branches that will burn for a long time. The wood must be dry and seasoned, otherwise it will smoulder or smother the fire. Have all these piles of wood to hand. If you've already amassed a pile of twigs, branches, hedge trimmings and other goodies where your bonfire stands, you'll have to dismantle it so you start building the bonfire from scratch. This will give any creatures that are sheltering in it a fighting chance of escape.

If you aren't confident of your fire-lighting skills, or the kindling is slightly damp, you might need some dry newspaper as well. If using the newspaper, crumple it up and place it on the ground first. If you have some dry wood shavings, put these on top of the newspaper. Arrange some of the kindling on top, in a crisscross pattern. This will ensure an adequate airflow on which the flames can feed, and will also keep the bonfire stable: you don't want it to fall over.

✎ Lighting the fire ✎

When you're ready, set light to the edges of the newspaper, or the kindling, with some matches. Chuck the spent matches into the fire and keep the box of matches well away from the flames. Be prepared to get down on your hands and knees to puff away at the tiny flames or glowing embers, to get them flaring into life. As soon as you have flames, you must feed them with wood or they'll eventually go out.

Gradually begin to build up the bonfire by putting on more small twigs, then larger ones and, finally, branches. Keep pushing large items into the heart of the fire, so it has plenty to feed on. Every now and then, using a hoe or garden fork, push the unburnt material from the edges of the bonfire into the middle, but always do this safely. If you want to burn green material, such as long grass or hedge trimmings, add them in small amounts once the fire has really got going to prevent them smothering the fire or creating a thick plume of acrid smoke.

≈ Controlling the fire ≈

Keep checking the perimeter of the bonfire to make sure the surrounding area isn't smouldering. If you're worried about the bonfire spreading, heap the edges into the middle. You might even want to water the area around the edge of the bonfire to control the fire, especially during periods of hot, dry weather.

Finally, only leave the bonfire when it's safe to do so, and preferably when everything has been burnt. Sweep up any twigs and branches that have fallen out of the fire and put them on the dying embers, which may soon flare up again. Wait until the embers are completely cool before moving the ash to areas of the garden where it can act as a fertiliser. If you don't want to use the ash immediately, let it get cold and then scoop it into old plastic fertiliser or potting compost bags and leave them in a dry place until needed.

EDIBLE FLOWERS

Flowers aren't just for putting in vases. They can also taste delicious, although not every flower is edible. Here is a selection of flowers that are good to eat, especially in salads. If you aren't sure about the safety of eating a particular flower, don't risk it because some are poisonous.

⇚ Chive flowers (*Allium schoenoprasum*) ⇛

Most of us pick chives and discard the flowers, but these are just as edible as the leaves. It may help to break them up into smaller florets. You can choose from traditional pink flowers, or those that are blue or white.

⇚ Courgette flowers (*Zucchini*) ⇛

These are a great delicacy when deep-fried in a light batter or stuffed. Pick them off the courgettes while they're still fresh. You can pay a fortune for these in smart greengrocers' so revel in the knowledge that they're plentiful and growing freely in your own garden.

⇚ Marigolds (*Calendula officinalis*) ⇛

Marigold petals taste delicious and look beautiful in salads, and add a peppery flavour and lovely yellow colour to risottos. Give the flowerheads a quick wash in some cold water, then pull off the petals and scatter these on your food; discard the rest of the flower. You can mash a few petals into cream cheese, too, for pretty sandwiches.

⇚ Nasturtiums (*Tropaeolum majus*) ⇛

Nasturtium flowers have a delectable peppery flavour. Check them for blackfly after you've picked them, then give them a quick dunk in some cold water before decorating salads with them. Nasturtium flower buds taste especially good.

⇚ Pansies (*Viola x wittrockiana*) ⇛

The flowerheads look lovely when sprinkled in salads, but do check them for insect life first.

❧ Runner bean (*Phaseolus coccineus*) ❧

Runner beans were originally grown for their lovely flowers, long before anyone hit on the bright idea of eating the seed pods. Assuming you can bear to sacrifice some of the flowers (which, after all, turn into the beans for which you're growing the plants), they have a lovely bean-like flavour.

❧ Thyme (*Thymus* sp.) ❧

If your thyme has started flowering, don't despair. Cut off the flowering spikes and sprinkle the individual flowers and buds on salads.

❧ Violets (*Viola* sp.) ❧

Tiny violets look lovely if you brush them with beaten egg white and then dip them in icing sugar before decorating a cake with them. Alternatively, you can put the entire heads in salads.

GROWING HERBS

No garden should be without a collection of herbs, even if you've got to cram them into corners, grow them in a windowbox or line them up in pots by your back door. They attract beneficial insects (see pages 71–5), they act as companion plants (see pages 84–5), they look pretty, you can use them for medicinal purposes and, perhaps best of all, they add so much to your cooking. Regularly cutting the herbs keeps them fresh and reduces their tendency to flower, which means you can enjoy their leaves for longer. If you have a large garden you can have fun creating a wonderfully diverse herb garden. But if you're short of space, which herbs should you grow? Here are ten of the best.

❧ Basil (*Ocimum basilicum*) ❧

What would a tomato salad be without basil? This fleshy, sun-loving tender annual is a valuable addition to any garden or windowbox, especially when you consider how much it costs to buy a bunch of fresh basil in the shops. There are lots of varieties to choose from, from Greek basil (*Ocimum basilicum*) with its tiny leaves and a pungent flavour, to lettuce leaf basil (*O. b.* 'Crispum'), which has enormous, crinkly leaves. Unfortunately, basil is not only a favourite of humans but of slugs and flea beetles, so you need to maintain a steady supply, preferably by sowing the seeds at regular intervals throughout the spring and summer.

❧ Chives (*Allium* sp.) ❧

It's easy to grow chives from seed. Although they take time to get established you will have them for many years, so it's worth the effort. You can grow ordinary chives (*Allium schoenoprasum*), with their mild onion flavour, or garlic chives (*A. tuberosum*) that taste just as you would expect from their name. Chives die back in winter but burst forth again the following year, and are at their best in early summer before the sun starts to stunt their growth. They need plenty of moisture without being drowned. Chopped chives add a wealth of flavour to salads, potatoes, egg dishes and sandwiches, and their round, edible flowers both look and taste good in salads.

❧ Coriander (*Coriandrum sativum*) ❧

It's so easy to grow coriander from seed that it would be a shame not to find a home for it somewhere in your garden. What you must bear in mind is that it bolts shamelessly, especially in hot weather, so you need a continual production line to ensure that there is always plenty of coriander to pick. If you cut off the top leaves of the plants, rather than cutting them off at the base, they will grow again. Coriander is a tender annual, but earns its keep in two ways because if you allow a few plants to just do what comes naturally you'll be able to harvest

plenty of coriander seed, which is fabulous when ground into curries and other spicy dishes. Coriander leaves add a wonderfully warm, aniseed-like fragrance and freshness to spicy foods, but are also delicious in salads.

❧ Lovage (*Levisticum officinale*) ❧

Lovage isn't as popular as it once was, which is a shame because it's a marvellous herb. Not only does it add a wonderful depth of aniseed-cum-fennel-cum-celery to cooked dishes (especially lentil dishes and vegetable risottos), it is also highly decorative in the garden. It isn't a herb for a small pot because it grows so large. Instead, it's perfect for filling a corner of the vegetable garden with its tall stalks covered with glossy, deeply lobed leaves. It's a herbaceous perennial, which means it dies back in the winter. You'll know that spring has truly arrived when you see it pushing its way out of the soil again.

❧ Mint (*Mentha* sp.) ❧

You can eat mint raw in salads, add boiling water for the most refreshing mint tea imaginable, make it into mint sauce to accompany roast lamb, turn it into mint jelly, add it to fruit salads or drop it in your glass of Pimm's. There are many different varieties, from the pretty, green and white apple mint (*Mentha suaveolens*) to the pungent spearmint (*M. spicata*). It can be very invasive, so unless you want it to colonise your garden you may prefer to grow it in a container or to restrict its roots in some other way. Unlike many other herbs, mint likes moist conditions so you must keep it well watered, especially if it's in a pot.

✑ Parsley (*Petroselinum crispum*) ✑

Rich in vitamin C, parsley is one of those must-have herbs. It's a biennial, which means that it seeds and then dies in its second year, so it's relatively short-lived. But don't let that put you off because it has endless uses in the kitchen, and if you grow it yourself there is no need to be sparing with it. Chop it finely and add to buttery new potatoes, use it in salads (especially in winter when it valiantly keeps on growing despite the weather), add it to a white sauce to accompany fish, put it in a stuffing or mix it with butter and shape into little pats to put on grilled meat. It's also a perfect breath-freshener, especially if you have a chronic garlic habit. Be patient if you're sowing it from seed because it can take ages to germinate – it helps to pour boiling water on the seeds and leave them for about an hour before sowing.

✑ Sage (*Salvia* sp.) ✑

This is the perfect herb to add to stuffings, but it's also wonderful in many Italian dishes and it gives plenty of flavour to those made from beans and lentils. Sage takes quite a lot of cooking to bring out its warm, aromatic flavour, so it's not something to add at the last minute because you won't get the most out of it. Possibly the most decorative variety is *Salvia officinalis* 'Tricolor', which is a wonderful mixture of purple, green and white. Whichever variety you have, sage needs a warm, dry situation and, if it's happy, will soon grow into a small shrub. Keep it well trimmed to stop it getting woody, and strike cuttings to create new plants every two or three years. Sage loses its pungency in winter when robbed of the sun's heat, so it's a wise move each summer to cut plenty of leaves for drying so you can use them throughout the winter months.

⇜ Sorrel (*Rumex acetosa*) ⇝

It's difficult to buy fresh sorrel, which is one of the reasons to grow it yourself. Sorrel is a hardy perennial with spear-shaped leaves, and it forms large clumps. It has a fresh lemony flavour, so is lovely in salads but is also good in soups and sauces. Some people find it hard to digest, and too much of it is thought to reduce the calcium in bones, so you must treat it with respect.

⇜ Sweet marjoram (*Origanum* sp.) ⇝

The scent of marjoram baking in the sunshine is so appetising that you'll be glad you've decided to grow it. It comes from the Mediterranean so thrives in hot, dry conditions. The tiny, spear-shaped leaves are best when added to dishes at the last minute to preserve their flavour, but they have a lot more pungency when dried. They are a classic addition to pizzas, and they're delicious in bean, rice or pasta salads.

⇜ Thyme (*Thymus* sp.) ⇝

This is a very pungent, aromatic herb with many different uses. It's one of the great culinary herbs, with tiny, oval, evergreen leaves and pretty flowers. It likes a dry, sunny situation and is fully hardy. Lemon thyme (*Thymus citriodorus*) is delicious, especially in salads and on new potatoes. Although thyme is a perennial it's not worth picking in the winter because its leaves don't have much flavour, so it's best to dry sprigs of it during the summer while they're plentiful.

COMPANION PLANTS

Clever gardeners have known for a long time that some plants are good companions, while others dislike being in close proximity to one another. You can use this knowledge to your advantage by putting friendly plants together, or using one plant to deter insects from landing on another. It's an especially useful system when growing herbs, vegetables and fruit.

Plant	Likes	Dislikes
Apple	Chive, nasturtium	Potato
Asparagus	Parsley, tomato	Onion
Basil	Bean, cabbage, tomato	
Borage	Strawberry, tomato	
Broad bean	Calendula, savory	Leek
Broccoli	Bean, nasturtium, potato	Leek, lettuce, strawberry, tomato
Brussels sprout	Bean, potato, sage	Strawberry
Cabbage	Beetroot, hyssop, rosemary	Strawberry, tomato
Carrot	Bean, pea, tomato	Dill
Cauliflower	Celery, nasturtium, radish	Strawberry, tomato
Chive	Carrot, parsley, tomato	Bean, pea
Courgette	Bean, nasturtium, sweetcorn	Potato
Cucumber	Bean, broccoli, tomato	Sage
Dill	Cabbage, lettuce	Fennel, carrot
Garlic	Carrot, tomato	Bean, pea, strawberry

Plant	Likes	Dislikes
Grape	Blackberry, bean	Cabbage, radish
Leek	Carrot, celery	Broad bean, broccoli
Lettuce	Beetroot, pea, strawberry	
Lovage	Bean	
Marjoram	Carrot, tomato, sage	
Mint	Cabbage	Parsley
Onion	Cabbage, carrot, lettuce	Bean, pea
Oregano	Cabbage, cucumber	
Parsley	Carrot, tomato	Mint
Pea	Carrot, cucumber, spinach	
Pear	Currants	
Pepper	Basil, onion, oregano	Fennel
Potato	Bean, lettuce, marigold, radish	Rosemary, tomato
Radish	Cabbage, lettuce, pea, tomato	Hyssop
Raspberry	Tansy	Blackberry, potato
Rosemary	Cabbage, carrot	Potato
Runner bean	Borage, carrot	Beetroot
Spinach	Cabbage, celery, onion	
Strawberry	Bean, lettuce, spinach	Broccoli, cabbage
Thyme	Broccoli, potato	
Tomato	Broccoli, cabbage, parsley	Fennel, potato

MAKING A SCARECROW

Farmers have been using scarecrows to frighten off birds for centuries. But they don't have to be confined to country fields because you can make a scarecrow for your own garden. Scarecrows are also reputed to deter herons from helping themselves to the fish in your pond. However, the birds will soon get used to the scarecrow if it's always in the same place, so be prepared to keep moving it around the garden.

Making your own scarecrow is a great way of using up tatty old clothes that are too grotty to give to your local charity shop or jumble sale – the birds won't care if they're full of holes or hideously out of fashion. It's also great fun. So, what do you need to make a scarecrow?

- Old jumper
- Old pair of trousers
- A large paper or plastic bag or an old pillowcase
- Straw, old plastic bags, newspaper or shredded paper
- Two bamboo garden canes or straight branches, one longer than the other
- String
- Needle and thread
- Scissors
- Thick felt pen

Choose the longer cane for the body and the shorter one for the arms. Make sure that the longer cane is sturdy enough to support the weight of the scarecrow when it's pushed into the ground.

Fill the paper or plastic bag, or pillowcase, with some of your chosen stuffing until it's head-shaped. Push the top of the long cane into the head, then bind the head to top of this cane with the string. If you're feeling artistic, you can draw a face on the front of the head. But don't worry if you don't do this because the birds are unlikely to notice.

Thread the shorter cane through the arms of the jumper, then bind the two canes together where they cross. With the scarecrow lying down, fill the jumper with your chosen stuffing and sew up the ends of the sleeves. Cut a small hole in the crotch of the trousers, then thread the long cane through this hole. Stuff the trousers from the waist down and the legs up, then sew up the end of each trouser leg to hold in the stuffing. Now baste the bottom of the jumper to the top of the trousers.

Your scarecrow is now ready to stand in your garden. But make sure you know where he is, otherwise you might mistake him for an intruder one night and scare yourself half to death.

TURNING ANIMAL MANURE INTO FERTILISER

A nimal manure can make great fertiliser, but some types are better than others. For instance, there is a long-standing tradition in country districts for keen gardeners to rush outside with a bucket and shovel whenever a horse passes, so they can collect any dung that's lying on the road. In time, this will rot down into a lovely, friable fertiliser for the garden. But the dung from a cat or dog has no value because it will go mouldy long before it rots down into anything useful. Some manures are pongier than others, as well. Pig manure is especially potent, so try to keep the maturing heap well away from the rest of the garden or your favourite seating area.

❧ Give it time ❧

Fresh animal manure should never be added directly to the soil because as it breaks down it will draw far more nutrients out of the soil than it puts in. It will also scorch the roots, stems and leaves of any plants that come into contact with it. Store it in a heap and cover this with some plastic sheeting or an old carpet to speed up the action of all the bacteria that will eventually break it down. Don't make the heap too large because these have been known to catch fire when the temperature inside them becomes too intense. Leave the heap to rot down for at least six months before you use the fertiliser.

If you have a compost heap you can add a small amount of the fresh manure to it, as this will act as an accelerator. You must still give it plenty of time to break down, though.

∼ Suitable manures ∼

Horse or donkey manure

Chicken manure

Rabbit droppings

Cow pats

Goat manure

Pig manure

CREATING A COMPOST HEAP

If you have a garden and you want to grow things in it, you need a compost heap, if not two or three if you've got enough space. It's a good idea to have more than one heap on the go at any time, so you can keep adding to the first while the second is maturing. All the microbes and other organisms in the compost heap will create heat, turning what was a lot of kitchen and garden waste into the most wonderful, dark, crumbly compost that will enhance your soil in many ways.

Making a compost heap is a lot easier than it might seem, but there are a few golden rules to follow if you want to be successful.

∼ Finding the right home ∼

The first rule is to situate the compost heap in a warm, sheltered part of the garden. Don't be tempted to hide it behind the potting shed where all that damp moss grows, or in a shady corner of the garden that's not fit for anything else, because none of the organic matter you put into the compost heap will rot down properly and it will simply turn sour. Just as you will when you discover the sorry mess you've made. If you're worried about the compost heap looking like an eyesore, you can always camouflage it by erecting a little fence in front of it. Alternatively, you can buy or build a smart wooden structure that you can boast about to your friends.

Prepare the ground by chopping down any perennial weeds that are growing there, such as stinging nettles. Don't worry about digging out the roots because the compost heap will soon kill off the plants by smothering them. However, you may want to dig up any brambles because these can be very resilient and you don't want to catch your skin or clothes on them.

❧ Making the structure ❧

If you're going to take composting seriously, you may wish to make a permanent structure for your heaps, such as bins made from wooden slats or small-gauge chicken wire lined with sheets of old wood. These structured heaps hold the heat well, but you can be almost as successful with a compost heap that's just piled up in one place.

❧ What can you compost? ❧

A great many things can go on a compost heap, and some of them are quite surprising. Compost heaps are the perfect destination for the peelings and other discarded bits from vegetables and fruit. It helps to cut these up small, to increase the surface area that's available for bacteria so that everything rots down more quickly. You can compost lots of things from the garden, too, such as clumps of annual weeds, some perennial weeds (but not their roots and not if they're setting seed), grass cuttings, unwanted seedlings, dead flowerheads and spent compost from old flowerpots. Some plants, such as stinging nettles, borage and comfrey, are pure gold for compost heaps because they add to the nutrition and texture of the finished product. If you

become fanatical about composting everything you can get your hands on, you can add really troublesome perennial weeds, such as ground elder and couch grass, if you leave them in a bucket of cold water for a few days first to kill them off. They won't smell very good but they'll now be a suitable addition to the compost heap.

Among the more surprising items you can add are tea leaves, tea bags (but slash them in half first), strips of newspaper, strips of cardboard, strips of old fabric (but nothing containing man-made fibres) and chopped-up knitting wool (again, no man-made fibres).

❧ What can't you compost? ❧

When adding vegetables and fruit from the kitchen, make sure they're all raw to avoid attracting rats and other pests. Some people never add potato peelings in case these carry disease, and some also avoid citrus peelings as these can be very acidic. Never add raw or cooked bones, meat, fish, eggs, dairy products and similar goodies otherwise the compost heap will be heaving with contented rodents instead of happy bacteria.

You should also avoid putting on anything too woody, such as prunings, hedge trimmings and branches, as these will take a very long time to rot down. The same is true of leaves from trees, so put these in a large black plastic sack, with a few air holes punched in it, to rot down and form a lovely leaf mould in a year's time.

It may sound obvious, but you can't add anything that won't rot down, such as plastic or metal. Well, you can add it but it will still be there when the rest of the compost is ready and you'll only have to sift it out again.

❧ Layers ❧

One of the great secrets of making a compost heap is to add the organic material in relatively thin layers, preferably varying the content of these layers as much as possible. Really dedicated composters collect the organic material in separate bins before assembling it in layers in the heap, so they have one bin for grass cuttings, another for vegetable waste, another for weeds, another for used soil, and so on. They then assemble the heap in layers, rather like making a lasagne.

Avoid adding too many grass cuttings at any one time because these can turn into a brown, soggy mess that, when it dries out, becomes an impenetrable mat that refuses to break down.

It's a good idea to cover the compost heap with sheets of cardboard or old carpet to keep in the heat and moisture.

❧ Turn and turn again ❧

You need to get moisture and air into the compost heap, so water it in dry weather and turn it on a regular basis to mix things up. This is hard work but worthwhile. Heft it all out on to the grass, into a wheelbarrow or into the next empty compost bin, then put it all back so what was on the top of the heap is now on the bottom. The aim is to aerate the mixture and to amalgamate things that are slow to rot down with those that are further along the decomposition route.

❧ Accelerators ❧

Some gardeners swear by accelerators that speed up the process of decomposition. You can buy various accelerators in garden centres, or you can create your own by adding some urine every now and then. No, it doesn't smell, and it works wonders.

WORMY FACTS

Children are often told not to worry when worms are accidentally chopped in half with a garden spade. Instead of dying, they will become two new worms. But is this true?

Generally speaking, no. Earthworms only have one mouth, which means that one half of the truncated worm will be able to carry on feeding (assuming that it doesn't die from shock after the injury), but the other half will eventually starve to death. However, if your spade went through the pink segment (the 'saddle') of the worm, which is where all its vital organs are stored, it may not survive at all.

Earthworms are surprising creatures. For instance, they can live for up to ten years, and have enormous strength that enables them to burrow into the soil. They're hungry, too, and eat their own weight every day. They're a gardener's best friend because they eat organic waste, and the worm casts they leave when they excrete their food are an excellent soil conditioner. Worms will break up soil for you without damaging its structure, whereas digging it yourself has the potential to do it – and you – harm.

Whatever the Weather

Rain, rain, go away,
Come again another day.

Traditional nursery rhyme

How to avoid being struck by lightning

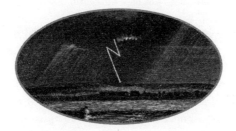

It looks dramatic when viewed from the safety of indoors, but lightning is a very different proposition when you're outside in the middle of a storm. It is even more dramatic, of course, but it's also a lot more dangerous. The temperature of a lightning bolt can be up to five times hotter than the surface of the sun, a fact that you may prefer to read about than to experience first-hand. Unfortunately, there is no failsafe way of avoiding a lightning strike, but if you want to reduce your chances of having it happen to you, here are some things to remember.

FIND SHELTER IMMEDIATELY! The best place is inside a solid structure, such as a house. However, this may still be struck by lightning, in which case the lightning will seek the fastest route to the earth. This means it will travel down electrical cables and water pipes, so it makes sense to switch off all large appliances, such as your television and computer, and unplug them at the wall. Avoid using the telephone, because this can also be a lightning conductor. Close the windows and doors, and keep away from them.

LISTEN AND COUNT How far away is the lightning? The best way to tell is to count the seconds between seeing the lightning flash and hearing the thunder. An interval of less than thirty seconds means there is a threat of being struck by lightning.

STOP DRIVING If you are in a car during a storm, it is advisable to park in a safe place (but not on the hard shoulder of a motorway). Close the windows and doors, and don't touch the doors, steering wheel, gear stick or anything else that could act as a lightning conductor.

KEEP AWAY If you're stranded outside with no immediate shelter in sight, there are still ways to increase your safety. Get away from high ground, open fields, exposed situations, trees, electricity pylons and sub-stations, telegraph poles, mobile phone masts and anything else that could attract a lightning strike. Keep away from water, too, such as the sea, a swimming pool, lake or pond. Put plenty of distance between you and anything metallic. Even if you're out in the pouring rain, you should get rid of your umbrella because the metal spokes could act as lightning rods. If you're on a golf course, abandon your golf clubs for the same reason. If you're fishing, put down your fishing rod and get away from the water.

OUT IN THE WOODS If you're in a wood or forest when a storm begins, you should avoid standing next to any very tall trees; shorter trees are a much safer proposition. If you have a choice, keep away from oak, elm and pine trees, all of which are most frequently struck by lightning. Folklore states 'avoid the ash, it courts the flash', so it would be wise to take this advice, too.

SEPARATE If you're caught outside with a group of people, you must all spread out so you are at least 20 feet away from one another. Switch off your mobile phones. Crouch on the ground, putting your feet together, kneeling down and tucking your head between your knees. Stay like this until the storm is over.

WAIT FOR IT TO PASS Wait for at least thirty minutes after the last clap of thunder before venturing outside again or continuing your journey, to make sure that the storm has passed. Every year, people are killed by lightning because they think a storm is over when it isn't.

HOW TO PREDICT THE WEATHER

If you ever listen to the weather forecast telling you that it's going to be a fine day, while watching the rain pour down outside, perhaps it is time to become your own weather forecaster.

Country folklore has plenty to say on the subject (see pages 101–3), but you can also predict the weather by looking at the sky and noticing what's happening around you.

❧ Clouds ❧

One of the best ways to predict the weather is to examine the clouds in the sky because they will tell you about changes in the weather. Clouds are formed when rising air becomes saturated with water vapour and condenses. There are four types of cloud – cirrus (white, wispy and very high), cumulus (mid-level, white or grey and heaped), nimbus (rain clouds) and stratus (layered clouds). Meteorologists combine these to create a list of cloud shapes, some of which denote fine weather while others warn of approaching rain – or worse. They form three groups, according to their height above the ground.

❧ High clouds ❧

CIRRUS Fragmented, white, wispy curls of ice crystals. They usually occur in fair weather. No rain.

CIRROCUMULUS Small, wispy, white blobs. When seen in the winter in northern latitudes they indicate cold but fine weather. No rain.

CIRROSTRATUS A widespread layer of cloud which may or may not obscure the sun or moon. A halo is often visible around the sun or moon. These clouds tend to thicken into altostratus when a warm front approaches. No rain.

✎ Medium clouds ✎

ALTOCUMULUS Often referred to as a 'mackerel sky'. Ripples, waves or small puffs of white or grey cloud. May also be accompanied by coloured rings around the sun or moon. An indicator of approaching cold weather. When these clouds appear on humid summer mornings they often presage thunderstorms later in the day.

ALTOSTRATUS Uniform layers of white or grey cloud, with the sun barely visible through a glassy veil. Often an indicator of continuous rain or snow.

NIMBOSTRATUS A thick layer of dark, low-level cloud that produces continuous heavy rain, or snow if the air is cold enough.

✎ Low clouds ✎

STRATOCUMULUS Low, lumpy patches, or sheets of light or dark grey clouds. Often accompanied by light rain over coasts and hills. When accompanied by north winds, they indicate clearing skies and cool temperatures; from the south, they indicate showers; from the west, they indicate clearing skies; and from the east, they indicate stormy weather. High stratocumulus, as their name suggests, sit higher in the sky. These are sometimes mixed with cumulus. They rarely produce rain or snow.

STRATUS Low, white or grey cloud, which obscures the sun or moon when thick. There can be considerable rain over coasts and hills.

CUMULUS Scattered heaps of puffy white clouds with round tops and flat bottoms. Normally an indication of fair weather, although light showers are possible.

CUMULONIMBUS Massive, tall, heaped clouds. The top consists of ice particles, while the lower, dark segment contains water droplets. Sometimes the cloud is in the shape of an anvil, which is a sure indication of bad weather. Heavy rain, thunderstorms or hail – or all three! – often with squally winds.

❧ Other things to look for ❧

Observe the contrails (condensation trails) left by aircraft, too. The longer they're visible, the greater the amount of moisture in the upper part of the sky.

In addition, it helps to observe what's going on around you. Open-faced flowers, such as daisies, will begin to close up their petals before it starts to rain. Insects don't like getting wet so make themselves scarce whenever rain is on the way. If there are plenty of bees, wasps and butterflies around, you can be confident of fine weather. If they disappear, it means that rain is coming.

THE BEAUFORT WIND SCALE

When does a light breeze become moderate? And how strong is the wind during a storm? One of the best ways of judging the wind's speed is by observing what it's doing to the objects around you. But how, in the days when there were no high-tech gadgets, could you quantify what the wind was doing in ways that everyone would understand?

Enter Sir Francis Beaufort, a sailor in the British Navy, who created what is now called the Beaufort wind scale – a method of determining the force of the wind. It wasn't the first of its type (several people had devised wind scales, including Daniel Defoe), but it is the system that has endured. Beaufort first developed it as a way of making uniform entries in his own ship's log, but it was so successful and logical that in 1838 the British Navy insisted that it should be used on every ship. At first, the Beaufort scale only described how the wind was affecting the sea's surface, but it was later expanded to include its effects on land, too.

Number	Mph	Knots	Effects on land	Effects at sea
0 Calm	0–1	0–1	Smoke rises vertically	Sea like a mirror
1 Light air	1–3	1–3	Smoke drifts	Calm but rippled
2 Light breeze	4–7	4–6	Leaves rustle, wind vanes move, wind felt on face	Small wavelets
3 Gentle breeze	8–12	7–10	Leaves and twigs move constantly	Large wavelets, crests starting to break, white horses
4 Moderate breeze	13–18	11–16	Small branches move, dust and loose paper move	Small waves becoming longer, numerous white horses
5 Fresh breeze	19–24	17–21	Small trees sway	Many white horses, some spray
6 Strong breeze	25–31	22–27	Large branches sway, hard to use umbrellas, telegraph wires whistle	Larger waves, sea covered in white horses, some spray possible
7 Moderate gale	32–38	28–33	Whole trees in motion, hard to walk against the wind	Streaks of white foam from breaking waves
8 Fresh gale	39–46	34–40	Twigs break off trees, progress hindered	Moderately high and long waves, streaks of foam
9 Strong gale	47–54	41–47	Branches break off trees, slight structural damage	High waves, sea begins to roll, spray affects visibility
10 Whole gale	55–63	48–55	Trees uprooted, considerable damage	Very high waves with long crests, white surface to sea, rolling sea

Number	Mph	Knots	Effects on land	Effects at sea
11 Storm	64–72	56–63	Widespread damage	Extremely high waves that hide ships, poor visibility, long patches of foam
12 Hurricane	73–136	64 and over	Devastation	Sea completely white, air filled with spray and foam, very poor visibility

WEATHER LORE

Hundreds of years of folklore have given us many different sayings and methods for predicting the weather, some of which are more accurate than others.

❧ Predicting bad weather ❧

Red sky at night, shepherds' delight.
Red sky in the morning, shepherds' warning.

Haloes around the moon or sun mean that rain will surely come.

If the moon rises with a halo round, soon we'll tread on deluged ground.

Moss dry, sunny sky; moss wet, rain you'll get.

When smoke descends, good weather ends.

When bees stay close to the hive, rain is close by.

Flies will swarm before a storm.

When seabirds fly to land there truly is a storm at hand.

Predicting a change in the weather

Rain before seven, fine before eleven.

No weather is ill if the wind is still.

The sharper the blast, the sooner it's past.

Snow like cotton, soon forgotten.
Snow like meal, it'll snow a great deal.

Clear moon, frost soon.

A sun-shiny shower won't last half an hour.

Predicting fine weather

When spiders weave webs by noon
Fine weather is going to follow soon.

When dew is on the grass,
Rain will never come to pass.

Frogs will call before the rain
But in the sun are quiet again.

Forecasting by the season or date

If Candlemas Day [2 February] be fair and bright
Winter will have another fight.
If Candlemas Day brings cloud and rain,
Winter won't come again.

If Candlemas Day be dry and fair,
The half o' the winter's to come and mair;
If Candlemas Day be wet and foul,
The half o' the winter's gane at Yule.

A wet March makes a sad harvest.

If March comes in like a lion it will go out like a lamb.

Ash [in leaf] before the oak, the summer's a soak.
Oak before the ash, the summer's but a splash.

If April blows its horn
It'll bring forth hay and corn.

St Swithun's Day [15 July] if it do rain,
For forty days it will remain.
St Swithun's Day if it be fair,
For forty days will rain no more.

If St Bartholomew's [24 August] be clear,
A prosperous autumn comes that year.

If ducks do slide at Hallowtide [1 November],
At Christmas they will swim.
If ducks do swim at Hallowtide,
At Christmas they will slide.

Wind in the north-west on St Martin's Day [11 November]
There's a severe winter on the way.
Wind in the south-west on St Martin's Day
There it will remain till February, and a mild winter will be had.

If sun shines through the apple trees upon a Christmas Day,
When autumn comes they will a load of fruit display.

Coasting Along

This precious stone set in the silver sea

Richard II, William Shakespeare

MILES OF ISLES

They aren't called the British Isles for nothing. Thousands of islands are scattered around the British coastline, from tiny skerries (small rocky islets that are covered by the sea at high tide or in stormy weather) to large, inhabited islands.

❧ English islands ❧

The English coastline is liberally sprinkled with islands of all shapes and sizes. Here's a selection of some of them:

Canvey Island	Lindisfarne
Denny Island	Longships
Godrevy Island	Lundy
Hayling Island	St Michael's Mount
Isle of Wight	Thorney Island

ISLES OF SCILLY

This small archipelago of islands lies south-west of the tip of Cornwall. There are over a hundred islands and islets, but the five main islands are:

Bryher	St Mary's
St Agnes	Tresco
St Martin's	

FARNE ISLANDS

The number of islands visible depends on the state of the tide, but in all there are over twenty. They're richly populated by birds but no humans. They include:

Big Harcar	Longstone
Brownsman	Megstone
Crumstone	North Wamses
East Wideopens	South Goldstone
Elbow	South Wamses
Inner Farne	Staple Island
Knoxes Reef	West Wideopens

❧ Welsh islands ❧

Wales has plenty of islands as well, including:

Anglesey	Holy Island
Bardsey Island	Puffin Island
Caldey Island	Ramsey Island
Cardigan Island	St Margaret's Island
Flat Holm	Skokholm
Grassholm	Skomer Island

❧ Scottish islands ❧

Scotland's craggy coastline has over seven hundred islands, ranging from the large groups of islands in the Atlantic Ocean to the small islets in the Firths of Clyde, Forth and Solway.

SHETLAND ISLANDS

These islands lie north-east of Orkney. There are over three hundred islands and skerries in this archipelago, so here is a short list of some of them.

Bressay	Muckle Roe
Bruray	Papa Stour
East Burra	Trondra
Fair Isle	Unst
Fetlar	Vaila
Foula	West Burra
Housay	Whalsay
Mainland	Yell

ORKNEY

Orkney has over seventy islands but many are unsullied by human feet. Here are the islands that are currently inhabited, whether in large or small populations, or were inhabited until recently.

Auskerry	Papa Stronsay
Burray	Papa Westray
Eday	Rousay
Egilsay	Sanday
Flotta	Shapinsay
Gairsay	South Ronaldsay
Graemsay	South Walls
Hoy	Stronsay
Mainland	Westray
North Ronaldsay	Wyre

OUTER HEBRIDES

These islands form an archipelago off the north-west coast of Scotland. They consist of a collection of inhabited and uninhabited islands, including the following:

Baleshare

Barra

Benbecula

Berneray

Boreray

Ensay

Eriskay

Flodaigh

Fuday

Great Bernera

Grimsay

Harris

Hermetray

Killegray

Kirkibost Island

Lewis

Mealasta Island

Mingulay

Monarch Islands

North Uist

Pabbay

Ronay

Rosinish

St Kilda

Sandray

Scalpay

Scarp

Scotasay

Seaforth Island

Shiant Islands

Shillay

Soay Mor

South Uist

Taransay

Vallay

Vatersay

Wiay

INNER HEBRIDES

These islands form an archipelago off the north-west coast of Scotland. They lie between mainland Scotland and the Outer Hebrides. The Inner Hebrides consist of a collection of inhabited and uninhabited islands, including the following:

Ascrib Islands

Canna

Coll

Colonsay

Crowlin Island

Danna Island

Easdale

Eigg

Eorsa

Erraid

Gigha

Gometra

Inch Kenneth

Iona

Islay

Jura

Kerrera

Lismore

Longay

Luing

Lunga

Muck

Mull

Oronsay

Pabay

Raasay

Rum

Sanday

Scalpay

Scarba

Seil

Sell

Shuna

Skye

Soay

(South) Rona

Staffa

Tiree

Treshnish Isles

Trodday

Wiay

ISLANDS OF THE CLYDE

These comprise the fifth biggest group of Scottish islands, and they lie in the Firth of Clyde between Ayrshire and Argyll. There are over forty islands and skerries in the group, including:

Ailsa Craig

Arran

Burnt Islands

Bute

Davaar

Great Cumbrae

Holy Isle

Inchmarnock

Lady Isle

Little Cumbrae

Sanda

⚒ Northern Irish islands ⚒

Rathlin

⚒ Crown Dependencies ⚒

This is where it all gets very complicated. The Isle of Man, which sits in the Irish Sea, is a self-governing Crown Dependency. It isn't part of the United Kingdom, although the UK is ultimately responsible for its well-being. The Channel Islands lie to the west of the coast of Normandy in France. They're organised into the Bailiwicks of Jersey and Guernsey, which are Crown Dependencies. Only the larger islands are inhabited.

Isle of Man

CHANNEL ISLANDS

Alderney	Herm
Brecqhou	Jersey
Burhou	Jethou
Casquets	Lihou
Les Dirouilles	Minquiers
Ecréhous	Les Pierres de Lecq
Guernsey	Sark

WHAT ARE KIPPERS?

I f you were to go fishing for kippers, you wouldn't find them. You'd have to fish for herring, instead, because kippers are herring (*Clupea harengus*) that have been split, gutted, salted and smoked. No one can say when kippers were first eaten, because humans have been smoking food in order to preserve it for millennia. In Britain, kippers are a traditional ingredient of breakfast and high tea.

Just to confuse matters, a kipper is also the name given to male salmon and sea trout during the breeding season. (The females are known as 'shedders' while they're breeding.)

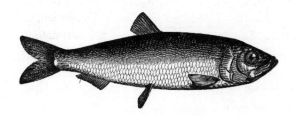

Herring were once so plentiful that, in their guise as kippers, they were the mainstay of the Scottish fishing industry and, therefore, of the Scottish diet. Herring were also fished extensively in Devon and Cornwall. They were known as 'silver darlings' because so many people earned their living from them. Fishing for them, however, was arduous in the days when it was done in open boats, and the fishermen would be at sea for long stretches while working in rough conditions. The women stayed by the harbour, working in the curing yards where they gutted the herring. This was fast and highly skilled work, with many women being able to gut sixty fish per minute. Nothing was wasted, because the fish guts were collected in barrels and used by farmers as fertiliser for their crops. The women worked extremely long hours because they couldn't stop until they'd processed the catch, otherwise it would spoil.

The traditional way to cure kippers is to wash the split and gutted fish before soaking them in brine. They are then hung on square wooden bars with hooks, known as 'kipper speets', with about eight kippers on either side. These are stacked in racks in the smoke house, where oak shavings and sawdust are smoking, and left for twelve hours. It's the oak shavings that give traditionally smoked kippers their deliciously subtle flavour.

FLOTSAM AND JETSAM

The sea washes all sorts of things on to the shore each day, from bits of seaweed to items that have fallen off ships. We often talk of random items being like 'flotsam and jetsam', but what does this actually mean?

Flotsam is the name given to items that float on the sea and have arrived there accidentally, such as goods that are washed overboard in a shipwreck or in bad weather. Jetsam, on the other hand, describes items that have been deliberately thrown overboard (jettisoned) in order to save the ship by lightening its load.

Lagan is another nautical term, describing wreckage that lies at the bottom of the sea.

LIGHTING UP THE COAST

Ever since we first put to sea in boats, we have needed something to warn us of dangerous stretches of coastline and to mark the entrances to ports. Originally, the best way to do this was to light fires on nearby hillsides, but eventually the idea of building something more solid and permanent was born. The Ancient Greeks built a few lighthouses, although nothing remains of them, and the Ancient Romans followed suit. Some of their lighthouses are still standing, including one of the pair that they built in the 1st century AD in Dover during their occupation of Britain. This pharos, as Roman lighthouses were called, can still be seen in the grounds of Dover Castle, where it's been adapted into the bell tower of the castle's chapel, St Mary de Castro.

❧ The role of Trinity House ❧

Britain's coastline is so rugged that it has long needed plenty of lighthouses to warn ships of possible dangers. In 1514 Henry VIII granted a royal charter to a group of mariners known as the Guild of the Holy Trinity, so they could regulate 'the pilotage of ships in the King's streams'. In 1566, Henry's daughter Elizabeth I commanded Trinity House to set up a system of beacons and other maritime warnings, and in 1609 Trinity House built its first lighthouse on the foreshore at Lowestoft.

Trinity House is still responsible for the building and maintenance of Britain's lighthouses. Today, lighthouses are all automatic so there is no need for them to be manned; in 1998 North Foreland lighthouse became the final automatic lighthouse when the keepers were withdrawn.

Every lighthouse is impressive, but here are some that have captured the public's imagination in some way.

❧ Beachy Head, Eastbourne, East Sussex ❧

With its red and white striped tower, and backdrop of chalk cliffs, this is one of the most easily recognisable lighthouses in the country. It stands below the headland known as Beachy Head (believed to be a corruption of the French *beau chef*, meaning 'beautiful headland') and east of the chain of chalk cliffs known as the Seven Sisters. The original Belle Tout lighthouse (built in 1828 by James Walker) stood on the headland, but its light wasn't visible in mist and cloud, so it had to be replaced. Beachy Head lighthouse was built from Cornish granite in 1902.

❧ Eddystone, Eddystone Rocks, Devon ❧

There has been a lighthouse on this dangerous stretch of rocks since the first wooden structure was lit for the first time on 14 November 1698. It was the first lighthouse to be built on a small rock in the open sea and began life as a private enterprise. It didn't last very long, being washed into the sea during the Great Storm of 1703. Its replacement, also wooden, caught fire in 1755. One of the lighthouse keepers, who was trying to put out the fire, swallowed some of the molten lead that was dripping off the lantern roof and later died of lead poisoning. The third lighthouse on this site was designed by John Smeaton and was a revolution in lighthouse design. He built it from granite blocks for strength, in the shape of an oak tree's trunk. Unfortunately, in 1877 it was discovered that although the lighthouse was sturdy enough, the rocks on which it was built were eroding. The fourth, and current, lighthouse stands next to the foundations of its predecessor. It was designed by Sir James Douglass, using the techniques and design that Robert Stevenson had developed from Smeaton's lighthouse. It was first lit in 1882 and, one hundred years later, it became the first fully automated lighthouse in Britain.

∾ Godrevy, St Ives Bay, Cornwall ∾

Godrevy lighthouse stands in St Ives Bay, in a stretch of sea that's a hazard to ships because of an underwater reef called the Stones. But Godrevy is best known for its association with Virginia Woolf, whose novel *To the Lighthouse* was inspired by memories of her childhood holidays in St Ives, even though she set the novel in the Hebrides.

∾ Longstone, Longstone Rock, Farne Islands ∾

This lighthouse, which was designed and built by Joseph Nelson in 1826, is famous for the events that took place here during a violent storm in September 1838. The steamer *Forfarshire* was wrecked on Hawkers Rocks, near the lighthouse, and the few survivors spent a terrible night clinging to part of its wreckage. The following morning, the lighthouse keeper, William Darling, thought the waves were still too rough to sail out and rescue the survivors, but his daughter,

Grace, insisted that they try. They managed to rescue nine survivors in two trips, and then had to find room for them in the lighthouse for two days until it was safe to take them ashore. William and Grace Darling became national heroes.

SUPERSTITIONS

From witches and wizards and longtail'd buzzards,
And creeping things that run in hedge bottoms,
Good Lord deliver us.

TRADITIONAL

How to Find Your True Love

Feeling lovesick or lonely? If you want to discover the identity of your true love, there are plenty of options to choose from, thanks to a wealth of folklore.

⮑ By the light of the silvery moon ⮐

If you are unmarried or without a long-term partner and you would like to know how long you must wait before Mr or Miss Right comes along, all you need is a clean silk handkerchief that has never been washed. Wait until the first new moon of the new year, then go outside when the moon is just a slender curve in the sky and look at it through the silk handkerchief. The number of moons you can see will tell you how many years you have to wait until the right person comes along. What you must not do is cheat and look at the moon through a window, because it's extremely unlucky to view a new moon through glass. Unfortunately, folklore is silent on whether this rule applies to those of us who wear spectacles.

While you are outside, shivering in the cold, you may as well make the most of it and follow this tradition too. Lean over the garden gate or fence and gaze at the moon, then recite this rhyme:

All hail to thee, moon, all hail to thee
I prythee good moon, reveal to me
This night who my husband [or wife] shall be.

Go back to bed, and you will dream of your future partner.

✐ Wedding cake ✐

Of course, if you're reading this in February you will have to wait for
the rest of the year before you can perform those January new moon
rituals, in which case you may be keen to try other traditional
methods. If you're lucky enough to be given a slice of wedding cake,
sleeping with it under your pillow (carefully wrapped up in grease-
proof paper, of course) will encourage dreams of your future beloved.
Alternatively, you could wake starving in the middle of the night and
scoff the lot.

✐ Hallowe'en customs ✐

Hallowe'en is the time of year when the veil between this world and
the next becomes very thin, which makes it an excellent opportunity
for some romantic detective work. If you've lit an open fire, you can
place one hazel nut for each prospective partner on the grate or
hearth. You then recite:

If you love me, pop and fly.
If you hate me, burn and die.

The nut that moves signifies which partner is in love with you.
You can also discover the initials of your future partner at
Hallowe'en. Peel an apple in one long strip, taking care that the peel
doesn't break. Then throw the peel over your right shoulder. Carefully
examine the shape that the peel forms when it lands because it will be
the initial of one of the names of your beloved.
There is another option, although it isn't for the faint-hearted. Sit

in front of your mirror, with only a candle to light the room, combing your hair while eating an apple. Look in the mirror and wait for the face of your future partner to appear over your shoulder.

∽ A Christmas Eve tradition ∽

In medieval times, a single girl who wanted to know the identity of her future husband would be busy on Christmas Eve baking what was called a 'dumb cake'. This was made from an eggshell of salt, another of wheatmeal and a third of barley. It was essential that the girl mixed and baked this in silence, and on her own. Having mixed up the cake, the girl would put it in the oven and leave the front door open. If everything went according to plan, her future husband would walk through the door at midnight.

HOW TO KEEP EVIL SPIRITS OUT OF YOUR GARDEN

Our country-dwelling ancestors lived in fear of the Devil and devised many ways of keeping him out of their houses and gardens. Here are some of the methods they used, in case you also want to keep Old Nick away from your hearth and home.

∽ Powerful trees ∽

Of course, you must begin outside by surrounding your home with plants that will repel evil and send a warning message to the Devil or any of the creatures in his thrall. The two most powerful trees for this are rowan (*Sorbus aucuparia*) and hazel (*Corylus avellana*). Rowan was always considered to be particularly good at combating evil, as some of its country names imply: it was called 'witchbeam' in Devon, 'witchwood' in Yorkshire and Cumbria, and 'witch-wicken' in Lincolnshire. Red is a good colour for repelling evil, so the rowan's crimson berries provide a warning to the Devil and his minions each autumn. Fairies and witches are said to be busy each May Day, so it made sense to pin rowan branches to the front door and even to tie rowan twigs to the milking pail, in case they tried to turn the milk sour. Hazel protects against evil spirits as well as malevolent fairies, and is traditionally brought inside the house, with rowan, on May Day.

Another tree that's always been believed to have extraordinary powers is the elder (*Sambucus niger*). However, it's traditionally been regarded with caution because the cross on which Christ was crucified was said to be made from elder wood (which is why it was once popularly called 'God's stinking tree' in Dorset). It is also said that Judas Iscariot, who betrayed Christ, hanged himself from the branches of an elder tree. While some people believed that elder protected them against witchcraft (especially on May Day when the leaves were particularly powerful) and were happy to have it in their gardens, others thought it was a wicked plant (it was known as the 'Devil's wood' in Derbyshire) and wanted nothing to do with it.

❧ Useful shrubs ❧

Have you ever noticed that many cottages have clumps of rosemary (*Rosmarinus officinalis*) growing by the garden gate or front door? You may think it's to release the rosemary's delicious scent whenever someone brushes past it, but traditionally it's because rosemary helps to protect against the evil eye.

Another useful plant is lady's mantle, which has been used to protect against elves for hundreds of years. Its Latin name, *Alchemilla*, means 'the little powerful one', in honour of its magical qualities.

Fennel (*Foeniculum vulgare*) often grows plentifully in gardens, which is just as well because it has long been used to keep ghosts at bay. In medieval times, it was one of the herbs hung over doorways to ward off evil spirits, and it could be stuffed into keyholes as well to stop ghosts passing through them. This makes it invaluable at

Hallowe'en, when there is little separation between the worlds of the living and the dead.

Don't forget to grow some garlic (*Allium sativum*), which is so useful for keeping vampires and other nasties away. Legend has it that when the Devil was cast out of the Garden of Eden, garlic grew in his left footprint and onion in his right.

WHICH WAY TO HANG A HORSESHOE

Horseshoes are plentiful in the countryside, for obvious reasons. They have been traditional decorations in homes for hundreds of years because of their alleged ability to bring good fortune, especially if they are hung over a doorway. But which way up should you hang your horseshoe?

If you hang it with the ends pointing upwards . . .
. . . tradition says that you're attracting good luck. What's more, you're holding the luck within the horseshoe, so it can't escape.

If you hang it with the ends pointing downwards . . .
. . . tradition is divided. Some authorities say the luck will drain out of the ends of the horseshoe. Others believe that this is the best way to hang a horseshoe, because the luck will cascade down on to you. Maybe you should experiment – if you dare.

FAIRY RINGS

How do you know if there are fairies at the bottom of your garden? Because you will see a fairy ring in the grass. This is a large circle that magically appears in the lawn, often apparently overnight, and then stays there. Sometimes the grass in the ring itself is taller than the grass around it, sometimes it's darker, and sometimes it dies off completely.

Children are often taught that these rings are made by fairies or elves. There are many traditional tales about them, including the theories that these are where fairies dance and that the circle marks the gateway to fairy realms deep inside the earth. Anyone who is acquainted with the legends surrounding fairies and elves will know better than to enter these subterranean realms themselves, in case they don't come back. It's equally dangerous to step inside the fairy ring, for fear of upsetting the fairies and dying young as a result. Neither should you walk widdershins (anticlockwise) around a fairy ring, because doing so will mean you fall under their power. In fact, there are so many folk traditions associated with the malevolence of these pretty rings that it might be best to keep well away from them. Assuming, of course, that you believe in such things.

The more prosaic explanation for fairy rings is that they're made by any one of possibly forty different species of fungus. Those that grow in grass, such as on your lawn, are called 'free' because the fungi aren't connected with any other organisms. The fairy rings that appear in forests and woods, however, are called 'tethered' because these fungi live in conjunction with the trees around them.

BIRD SUPERSTITIONS

People once thought that birds had a direct connection with God because they flew so high they were able to whizz in and out of Heaven. The Ancient Romans practised augury, which is a form of divination based on the flight and behaviour of birds. This helped to give rise to many superstitions about birds, many of which are still believed.

BLACKBIRDS Blackbirds are good news, and it's considered to be very fortunate if a blackbird makes a nest in your home. You can expect to receive some good luck if you see two blackbirds sitting together.

CHICKEN EGGS After eating a boiled egg, it's essential that you bash a hole through the bottom of the shell. If you don't, witches will go to sea in it so they can cast bad luck on sailors and sink their ships.

CUCKOO! When you hear the distinct call of the cuckoo it's one of the many signs that spring has finally arrived. Tradition has it that the cuckoo can be heard between St Tiburtius' Day (14 April) and St John's Day (24 June). If you hear a cuckoo singing on St Tiburtius' Day itself, you must turn over all the money in your pockets, while spitting and not looking at the ground. You'll enjoy good luck if you're standing on soft ground at the time, but bad luck will arrive if the ground you're standing on is hard.

IN THROUGH THE WINDOW It's always a bad sign if a bird flies into the house because it's the portent of a death. And that death will happen soon if the bird flies in through the window.

MAGPIES Magpies are generally regarded as unlucky birds because it was once thought that they were the Devil in disguise. Whenever you see a magpie, you should deflect any potential bad luck it brings by greeting it politely. You can also count the number of magpies you see, according to the traditional rhyme:

> *One for sorrow,*
> *Two for joy.*
> *Three for a girl,*
> *Four for a boy.*
> *Five for silver,*
> *Six for gold.*
> *Seven for a secret*
> *Never to be told.*

OWLS It's unlucky to see an owl in daylight. You don't want to hear an owl hooting before sunset, either, because it means that bad luck is on the way.

RAVENS Apparently, King Arthur visits the world in the form of a raven, so it's extremely bad luck to kill one.

ROBINS Make a wish as soon as you see the first robin of winter. Your wish will come true, provided that the robin doesn't fly away before you've finished making that wish.

SEAGULLS If you see three seagulls flying overnight, they warn of a death.

SPARROWS Never kill a sparrow because these are the birds that carry the souls of the dead. Another theory is that a sparrow sat beside Jesus during his crucifixion, so the birds are blessed and should therefore never be harmed.

SWANS Swans are monogamous, so sewing a swan's feather into the pillowcase of your beloved will ensure his or her fidelity to you.

VALENTINE'S DAY Women should keep a special lookout for birds in flight on Valentine's Day. If a woman sees a robin, it means she will marry a sailor. If she sees a sparrow, she'll marry someone poor who will make her happy. Best of all is if she sees a goldfinch because then she will marry a rich man.

OLD WIVES' TALES

We grow up hearing all sorts of old wives' tales. Some of them seem completely arbitrary and nonsensical, while there may be a grain of truth in others. Here's a selection of some traditional beliefs.

AVOID LILAC If you want to keep death away from your home, never bring lilac (*Syringa* sp.) into it, even though it smells and looks heavenly.

BASHING A GANGLION The traditional way of curing a ganglion (a collection of nerve fibres that form a lump, often on the hand) is to bash it hard with the family Bible. The idea is that force disperses the ganglion. But don't do it! Get your doctor's advice instead.

CATCHING COLD Going out into the cold with wet hair will make you catch a cold, according to old wives. In fact, it's viruses that give us colds, not wet hair.

CURING COUGHS As far as old wives were concerned, one good way to cure a cough was to pass it on to the faithful family dog.

They plucked a hair from the head of the person who was coughing, who then slapped it between two slices of bread and gave the sandwich to the dog, saying, 'Eat well, you hound. May you be sick and I be sound.'

HOW TO CURE HICCUPS It's so annoying when you get hiccups, especially when everyone around you starts laughing and your hics get louder and louder. Those old wives had a host of suggestions about how to stop your hiccups in their tracks. One idea was to drink a glass of water from its opposite side. This means tipping the glass away from you while trying to drink out of the other side, and it's practically impossible. Perhaps the idea was that you'd be so intent on sipping the water without drenching yourself in it that you'd forget to hiccup.

Shock tactics are another favourite remedy. One idea is to drop a cold key down the afflicted person's back. Sadists prefer to use an ice cube.

ITCHY PALMS If the palms of your hands itch, the old wives say it means that money is on its way to you. The one thing you mustn't do is to scratch that itch, because it will send the money away again.

MOUTH ULCERS According to the old wives, if you have an ulcer on your tongue it's because you've been telling lies.

NE'ER CAST A CLOUT TILL MAY IS OUT To translate, this means 'don't stop wearing your vest until the end of May'. There is a theory that 'May' refers to the hawthorn tree (*Crataegus monogyna*), whose common name is 'may', and therefore you should wait until the hawthorn is in blossom before putting your vests away. However, anyone with a good memory will know that it can get very cold in May and it's therefore unwise to dispense with your cosy underwear until June is in your sights.

NEVER PUT NEW SHOES ON A TABLE OR BED Old wives would have thrown their aprons over their heads in panic if they'd ever seen you put a new pair of shoes on a table or bed. Why? Because it will bring death into the house.

PEARLS FOR TEARS Engagement rings should never contain pearls, according to the old wives, because they look like tears and will therefore bring sorrow.

RINGING IN YOUR EARS If your ears start to ring, it's supposed to mean that someone is talking about you.

SALT AND THE DEVIL The next time you spill some salt you must act quickly. Throw a pinch of it over your left shoulder three times in quick succession and it will hit the face of the Devil.

FUN AND GAMES

Boys and girls come out to play,
The moon doth shine as bright as day.

TRADITIONAL NURSERY RHYME

How to make a fighting conker

For many children (and some adults), autumn wouldn't be the same without conkers. These beautifully shiny, dark brown fruits of the horse chestnut tree (*Aesculus hippocastanum*) can be quickly converted into the simple ingredients for the essential autumnal game of conkers.

The rules are straightforward. Each player prepares their conker by boring a hole through it with a metal skewer (taking care not to impale their hands at the same time), then threading it with a length of string that's knotted at one end. They then aim their conker at their opponent's, with the intention of hitting this so hard that it breaks.

Obviously, it pays to have a decent conker that will survive assaults by other players' conkers. But how do you choose the right one?

✑ Choosing a suitable conker ✑

First, don't go for quantity rather than quality. An autumnal walk in a park or wood will probably yield many conkers lying on the ground, having shed their prickly green casings, and it's tempting to pick the fattest, shiniest one you can see and to leave the rest for the squirrels. However, you must select your conker carefully because you want it to be as hard as possible. Collect a few of the heaviest conkers and take them home, then place them in a bucket of water. Those that float have internal damage and should be discarded. Those that sink are intact, solid and worth keeping. Fish them out of the water and leave them to dry on a towel. Strictly speaking, all you need to do next is to thread your conker and try your luck. That is the sporting option.

≫ Playing the game while not ≫ 'playing the game'

The cheating option, on the other hand, involves strengthening your conker. There are various ways to do this, all of which are illegal in the game of conkers. You can soak or boil the conker in vinegar or salt water, which will harden it up; soak the conker in paraffin; bake an unsoaked conker in the oven for about thirty minutes; or keep it in the dark for a year while it shrivels (although, admittedly, this is a bit of a giveaway). Not surprisingly, the conkers used each October at the World Conker Championships in Ashton, Northamptonshire, are supplied by the organisers, to avoid all doubts about any funny business.

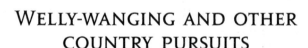

WELLY-WANGING AND OTHER COUNTRY PURSUITS

In some corners of the globe, Britain has the reputation for being a very eccentric country. And that is hardly surprising when you consider some of the ways people pass the time in the countryside. Some of these may look sweetly bucolic but don't be fooled. They can be pretty dangerous, too.

≫ Cheese-rolling ≫

Not for the faint-hearted! Cheese-rolling is a sport, since it involves rolling one large circular cheese down an extremely steep hillside, with lots of people chasing it down the precipitous slope and trying to catch it. In practice, they never do because as the cheese hurtles down the hill it can reach 110 kph (70 mph), which gives it enough force to knock over anyone who gets in its way. The first person over the finishing line wins the cheese. This may sound fairly easy but it's no picnic. Trying to keep your balance while hurtling head-long down the hill requires skill, not to mention an iron nerve and strong ankles.

Cheese-rolling has been practised in Cooper's Hill in the Cotswolds for at least two hundred years, if not longer. Some sections of Cooper's Hill are so steep that they have a 1:1 incline. Cheese-rolling here is now such a popular event that people come from all over the world each May to take part in the fun. The cheese in question is a locally made Double Gloucester.

∼ Egg-rolling ∼

This is an ancient British tradition that is particularly popular at Easter in Lancashire, Cumbria, Derbyshire and Scotland. It also goes by the name of 'pace-egging', from *pasch*, which is the Old English word for Easter. Sometimes, the game is accompanied by people dressed as mummers (people who used to travel around the country-side performing traditional plays). The eggs were originally wrapped in onion skins and boiled, which gave them an attractive appearance and ensured that they didn't break when they were rolled down hills. The aim is to see who can roll their egg the furthest.

∼ Egg-tapping ∼

Also practised at Easter, in many ways this is a variation of conkers but it uses hard-boiled eggs. Each contestant has a hard-boiled egg, and the aim is to tap your own egg against your opponent's in such a way that yours remains intact while your opponent's egg is smashed. Naturally, this can lead to cheating, such as using a marble egg. One obvious way to avoid this is for the winner to eat their own egg at the end of the game.

≫ Welly-wanging ≈

In theory, this is a much safer sport. It involves hurling a wellington boot as far as possible, from a designated starting position. It's believed to have originated in Yorkshire. An interesting variation is to flick the welly off the end of your foot and see how far it travels. You might like to get some practice at this the next time you come in from the garden wearing a pair of muddy boots that you can't bear to touch.

MAKING AND USING A FLOWER PRESS

Have you ever gone for a country walk, seen a pretty flower and picked it, and then wondered what to do with it? Have you ever been given a flower by a sweetheart and wished you could stop it withering away?

The Victorians knew all about pressing flowers to preserve them, and used them in many decorative ways. It is easy to do the same and you don't need much equipment. You can glue the finished results on handmade cards, bookmarks and notelets, or even have them framed.

If you expect to press lots of flowers in the future, you can buy a special flower press, but it's just as simple to improvise your own. You can always buy more specialist equipment later, if you get the flower-pressing bug. Here is what you need:

- Large sheets of clean blotting paper
- Some large, heavy books
- Flowers

Make sure you pick the flowers when they're at their best – there's no point in pressing anything that's been nibbled by insects, is losing its petals or is about to die. Immediately put the flowers in water to keep them fresh (it helps to take a bucket or vase of water with you when picking them, so that there's no delay in doing this). If the flowers are covered in dew or rain, you must wait for all the moisture to evaporate before pressing the flowers, otherwise they could go mouldy.

When you're ready to press the flowers, check that they aren't providing a home for any little insects. You can either detach the flowerhead from its stem, which you discard, or you can press the entire flower, leaves and stem. Some leaves, such as those of hardy geraniums, are very attractive, so are worth pressing. Open one of the heavy books and place a sheet of blotting paper on the lower page. Make sure it lies flat. Take the first flower and arrange it carefully on the blotting paper. Squish down the petals if you wish or fan out the leaves in an attractive shape. Arrange more flowers on the paper but don't let them touch one another. When you're ready, place another sheet of blotting paper on top of the flowers, making sure you don't move them in the process. Then carefully close the book and pile on some more heavy books. Leave them in a safe place for at least four weeks before inspecting the flowers to see if they're completely dry. Very thick, sappy flowers will take longer to dry than thin ones.

It may take a little practice to get into the swing of pressing flowers, so don't be disappointed if your first attempts aren't great. You will soon get the hang of it.

Pooh sticks

This timeless game was immortalised by A. A. Milne in his Winnie the Pooh books, and is worth playing even if you're supposed to be a sensible grown-up. It helps to have a child, or children, to join in but it's just as much fun with two or more adults.

All you need is a bridge, a running river or stream beneath it, and some large twigs. Each contestant chooses a twig of roughly equal length and thickness to all the others, for the sake of fairness. Look to see the direction in which the water is running, and stand on the opposite side of the bridge. Everyone drops their twigs into the water at the same time, and then rushes to the other side of the bridge to see whose twig emerges first.

This might sound simple, but it's astonishing how often a twig will get hooked in some weed or caught in a little eddy so it spins round and round while everyone else's twigs whizz past.

The rules of ferret racing

Poor old ferrets. You can't help feeling sorry for them when you know how they have to race. Three ferrets are pitted against each other in each race. The proud owner (or perhaps that should be 'trainer') of each ferret has to persuade the little creature to run through a length of pipe. This, of course, is a lot trickier than it sounds since ferrets don't always play by the rules, and can fail to appreciate the fact that money or family honour may be riding on the result, so they may dally on their journey or even decide to go on strike. What's more, as soon as the ferret has finally reached the other end of the pipe, it has to go all the way back again. At this halfway stage, the owner is allowed to pull the ferret out of the pipe, turn it round and shove it back in again, before persuading it to retrace its journey through the pipe to the original starting line.

This time, when the ferret reaches the end of its return journey, the owner isn't allowed to touch it until it's emerged completely and its tail is clear of the pipe. This can take some time, presumably because the ferret has other things to think about than the outcome of the race.

MORRIS DANCING

What's the most dangerous thing about morris dancing? The risk of falling off the bonnet. (Think about it.)

Forget any association with morris dancing and Morris Minors. Morris dancing has a long tradition in Britain although, as with so many other practices that are woven into the fabric of the country, no one is entirely sure when morris dancing began or where it came from. There are various theories on this subject: that it evolved from Spanish dancing (originally called 'moorish' dancing); that it is entirely home-grown, having evolved from medieval courtly dances; and that it's a form of fertility dance.

Regardless of where it originated, people in Britain have been morris dancing for hundreds of years. It was a great favourite of Henry VII, and in 1494 his court made its first payment to the performers of a 'Morrice Dance'. Henry's son, Henry VIII, was also a fan of morris dancers and they often entertained his court. By this time, though, the dancing was taking place up and down the country and not only in aristocratic settings.

The clothes and other accoutrements are an essential ingredient in morris dancing. Different groups may wear slightly different outfits so each has its own particular identity, but the men often wear trousers with ribbons tied around the thighs, calves or ankles, and with more ribbons tied around their arms. The women often wear blouses and long skirts. Some morris groups wear bells, too, which jingle as they move.

There are six forms of morris dancing in Britain, each of them named for a particular part of the country and with its own specific style of dance. Some of these styles are flourishing while others are thought to be in decline.

❧ Border ❧

This is derived from Herefordshire, Worcestershire and Shropshire, which are all on the England–Wales border. The dancers often colour their faces to confer anonymity, and they have a characteristically loose, relaxed style of dance. They wear 'rags', which are clothes completely covered in strips of ribbon and rag that move as they dance. The sides consist of four, six, eight or twelve men.

❧ Cotswold ❧

This is a style of dance from parts of Gloucestershire, Oxfordshire and Northamptonshire. The dancers carry handkerchiefs and wave sticks. There are six dancers and a musician, and sometimes there's a Fool or some sort of animal character. The dress is quite restrained.

❧ Longsword ❧

Longsword dancing derives from Yorkshire and is closely related to rapper sword dancing. The 'swords' are made from wood or rigid metal. Six or eight men dance in a circle, each holding on to his neighbour's sword throughout the entire dance. They don't wear bells.

✎ Molly dancing ✎

This style of dancing comes mainly from the East Midlands and East Anglia. The dancers often blacken their faces with soot. Traditionally they were all men, with one man dressed as a woman (the molly). Today, molly dancing is performed by men and women.

✎ North West morris ✎

This style of morris dancing originated, as its name suggests, in north Cheshire and north Lancashire. It's performed by at least nine men and women, and takes the form of a processional dance. The dancers wear wooden clogs fitted with irons that accentuate the rhythm of their dancing.

✎ Rapper ✎

This has nothing to do with modern music, but is named after the rapper swords that are such a distinctive feature of this style of dance. It comes from Northumberland and Durham, and is performed by five dancers carrying short, flexible 'swords'. Sometimes the Fool characters join the dancers.

THE STARRY HEAVENS

The hornèd moon, with one bright star
Within its nether tip.

THE RIME OF THE ANCIENT MARINER,
SAMUEL TAYLOR COLERIDGE

SHINE ON, HARVEST MOON

In the days before written calendars, our ancestors had their own methods of keeping track of the months and seasons. One of the best was to note the changing phases of the moon, with its new and full moons. A full moon happens once every twenty-nine days, which means that on average there is one moon a month (originally, this word was a 'moonth'). How simple, then, to give each month's full moon a name that was associated with the natural world at that particular time of the year. The names varied slightly from one region and culture to another, but here are some of the names that were – and still are – used in the northern hemisphere.

JANUARY	Wolf Moon
FEBRUARY	Snow or Ice Moon
MARCH	Worm or Storm Moon
APRIL	Pink or Growing Moon
MAY	Flower or Hare Moon
JUNE	Strawberry or Mead Moon
JULY	Buck or Hay Moon

AUGUST	Sturgeon or Corn Moon
SEPTEMBER	Harvest Moon
OCTOBER	Hunter's Moon
NOVEMBER	Beaver or Snow Moon
DECEMBER	Cold or Winter Moon

Two of these moons are especially important. The harvest moon is the full moon that appears closest to the autumn equinox (20 or 21 September), and the hunter's moon is the full moon that appears in the following month (October). Both are special because they rise on successive evenings more quickly than the other moons of the year. This means there is a shorter period of darkness between sunset and moonrise, so there is more light outside for farmers and hunters to do their work.

That's not the only reason why harvest and hunter's moons are important. They both look larger than other moons, and often a lot redder, too. They appear bigger because they hang lower in the sky, thanks to the Earth's tilt at that time of year, and they can look redder because the light of the moon is seen through the vast number of particles that are in the atmosphere closest to the Earth. So next time you admire a coppery harvest or hunter's moon, try not to let the fact that atmospheric pollution has turned it red detract from the romance of such a beautiful sight.

THE TWENTY-FIVE BRIGHTEST STARS IN THE NIGHT SKY

One of the great pleasures of being in the countryside is seeing the night sky studded with stars. It's the planets and the brightest stars that stand out. But which are the brightest stars? In the following list they're arranged in their order of magnitude, beginning with Sirius, the brightest star of all.

Name of star	Constellation	Popular name	Hemisphere
Sirius	Canis Major	The Great Dog	Both
Canopus	Carina	The Keel	Southern only
Arcturus	Boötes	The Herdsman	Both
Alpha Centauri	Centaurus	The Centaur	Both
Vega	Lyra	The Lyre	Northern only
Capella	Auriga	The Charioteer	Both
Rigel	Orion	The Hunter	Both
Procyon	Canis Minor	The Little Dog	Both
Achernar	Eridanus	The River	Both
Hadar	Centaurus	The Centaur	Both
Betelgeuse	Orion	The Hunter	Both
Acrux	Crux	The Southern Cross	Southern only
Altair	Aquila	The Eagle	Both
Aldebaran	Taurus	The Bull	Both
Antares	Scorpio	The Scorpion	Both
Spica	Virgo	The Virgin	Both
Pollux	Gemini	The Twins	Northern only
Fomalhaut	Piscis Austrinus	The Southern Fish	Both
Deneb	Cygnus	The Swan	Northern only
Mimosa	Crux	The Southern Cross	Southern only
Regulus	Leo	The Lion	Both
Adhara	Canis Major	The Great Dog	Both
Castor	Gemini	The Twins	Northern only
Gacrux	Crux	The Southern Cross	Southern only
Shaula	Scorpio	The Scorpion	Both

CELESTIAL NAVIGATION

People have been navigating with the help of the stars in the night sky for millennia, and it's still an excellent way of getting your bearings. This means, of course, that you will have to find other ways of working out directions on nights when it's too cloudy to see the stars.

Even if you have no reason to use celestial navigation, it's good fun and you'll get used to looking up at the night sky and finding your way around it. This method enables you to find north in the northern hemisphere.

≈ Watching the stars ≈

The stars appear to move around the sky each night, as you'll realise if you track the progress of a particular constellation during an evening. Some stars disappear over the horizon as the hours pass, while others begin to rise. Of course, it's not really the stars that are moving. Instead, it's the Earth that's spinning against the vast backdrop of the night sky.

≈ The north celestial pole ≈

If you're in the northern hemisphere, you will be able to locate north by looking in the sky for the stars nearest the north celestial pole. If you're in the southern hemisphere, you can locate south by looking for the stars nearest the south celestial pole. These celestial poles are imaginary extensions of the Earth's North and South Poles. Try visualising a huge skewer going through the Earth's poles and sticking out either side – the two ends are the celestial poles.

The nearest star to the north celestial pole (and therefore known as the north star) is Polaris, so this is what you must locate if you want to find north.

☙ Locating Ursa Major ❧

So how do you find the north celestial pole? Go outside on a starry night and look up into the sky at the stars. Switch off any outside lights, as well as indoor lights that shine into the garden. It can take a few minutes for your eyes to adjust to the darkness, especially if you've previously been in bright light, so be patient. As your eyes adjust you'll see an increasing number of stars. Now look for the Ursa Major constellation, also known as the Great Bear. It's a big, sprawling constellation that contains a small collection of stars variously known as the Plough and the Big Dipper. The Plough consists of seven stars, with four arranged in a rectangle that looks like a cup and three forming a convex tail that looks like a curved handle. These stars are always visible somewhere in the night sky in the northern hemisphere. The top star on the leading edge of the cup (the side furthest from the handle) is pointing directly towards the north star, Polaris. However, depending on where you live, you may not be able to see Ursa Major very clearly in the autumn and winter unless you have an uninterrupted view of the northern horizon.

☙ Locating Cassiopeia ❧

If Ursa Major is too low in the sky, you can look instead for the constellation known as Cassiopeia, which sits on the opposite side of Polaris. Cassiopeia is always visible in the northern hemisphere and it's a very useful location device because it points to so many other stars and constellations. It's composed of five bright stars arranged in the shape of a 'W'. Look for the top left-hand star in the 'W', because that will be pointing directly towards Polaris.

⇜ Looking for Ursa Minor ⇝

If you want to confirm that you've actually found Polaris, look for Ursa Minor. It's known as the Little Bear because it's a mini version of the Great Bear, with four big stars arranged in a rectangle and three stars leading off it in a tail. The third star, forming the end of the tail, is Polaris. Bingo!

⇜ Locating north ⇝

True north lies just below Polaris, when you have Ursa Major to your left and Cassiopeia to your right. This means that west is to your left, east is to your right, and south is behind you.

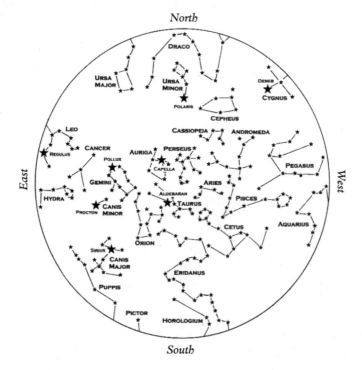

Starry stories

The beauty and mystery of the night sky are captivating, so no wonder our ancestors organised the stars into separate constellations and created legends around them. Here are some of the most interesting stories about a few of the constellations that we can still see today.

⇌ Andromeda ⇌

This is also known as the Chained Princess, because it's named after the Greek myth of Andromeda whose parents chained her to a rock by the sea as a sacrifice to the hideous monster Cetus. Luckily for Andromeda, Perseus rescued her on his winged horse, Pegasus, and turned Cetus to stone by showing him the severed head of the gorgon Medusa.

Andromeda is a constellation in the shape of a long, curved 'V' that's found near Cassiopeia (Andromeda's mother in Greek mythology). In the sky she's surrounded by constellations named after the other characters in her myth: Perseus, Pegasus and Cepheus (her father).

Andromeda contains a spiral galaxy that's the closest major galaxy to ours and is bright enough to be seen with the naked eye on a dark night.

⇌ Canis Major ⇌

This is the Great Dog, and unlike many constellations it still has the vague shape of what it purports to be. It's accompanied by Canis Minor (the Little Dog) that sits above it in the night sky. There are lots of charming legends connected with these dogs. One is that Canis Major is Laelaps, a dog that ran so fast it was able to win a race against a fox and was rewarded by Zeus with a place in the sky. Another legend is that the dogs belong to Orion, the great hunter, who strides through the nearby sky.

Canis Major contains Sirius, also known as the Dog Star, which is the brightest star in the night sky. It's over forty times more luminous than the Sun.

≈ Corona Borealis ≈

There is a lovely story connected with this constellation. It's known as the Northern Crown because it's a deep semi-circle of stars. Greek legend has it that the crown belongs to Ariadne, who was the daughter of King Minos of Crete. Ariadne didn't want to marry Dionysus because she thought he was a mortal, so he proved he was a god by hurling his crown into the sky. Won over by this romantic gesture, Ariadne married him.

≈ Hercules ≈

He's given his name to the concept of being strong, and Hercules was revered throughout the Mediterranean for his remarkable strength. It was Hercules who embarked on the twelve labours in order to prove himself. Although he was half-mortal, at the end of his life his father, Zeus, made him one of the gods and gave him a place in the sky.

Hercules is a big, sprawling constellation near Boötes, at the centre of which are four stars in a rough rectangle: Epsilon, Zeta, Eta and Pi.

≈ Orion ≈

The massive size and easily recognisable shape of Orion means that many civilisations have built legends around this striking constellation. To the Syrians, this was Al Jabbar or the Giant, and the Ancient Egyptians thought it was Sahu, the soul of Osiris. To the Greeks, this constellation represented Orion, the great hunter. When he was accidentally shot and killed by Artemis, she was so heartbroken that she placed his dead body in the sky, surrounded by his cherished hunting dogs (Canis Major and Minor). He holds a raised club in his left hand and a lion's pelt in his right, and he has a belt around his waist.

✻ Ursa Major ✻

This is also known as the Great Bear, and it's one of the most easily identified constellations in the night sky. This means there are many legends associated with it. The ancient Britons believed that the Plough, which is a small part of Ursa Major, was King Arthur's chariot. For the Greeks, Ursa Major is connected with Zeus, who had a son, Arcas, with Callisto, who was a mortal. Zeus's wife, Hera, was so jealous that she turned Callisto into a bear that was nearly killed by Arcas while out hunting. Perturbed, Zeus rescued Callisto and Arcas, and put them in the night sky out of harm's way. Callisto became Ursa Major and Arcas became nearby Ursa Minor.

SNUG INDOORS

'This,' said Mr Pickwick looking around him, 'this
is, indeed, comfort.'

THE PICKWICK PAPERS, CHARLES DICKENS

THE JOYS OF A LOG FIRE

Log fires and the countryside go together. A country cottage wouldn't be the same with an electric heater on which to toast your toes. You need a roaring fire, a comfy chair and, preferably, a toasting fork with which you can toast some crumpets or teacakes before smothering them in butter and eating them to keep your strength up. But, first, you've got light the fire, and that isn't always easy.

❧ Lighting the fire ❧

Before you start, it's important to make sure that the chimney has recently been swept and isn't clogged up with clinker, soot or birds' nests, otherwise the fire won't draw properly and the room will fill with choking smoke. Very short chimneys can also fail to draw well, although there isn't much you can do to get round this problem.

Empty the grate of any ash or debris from previous fires. Set aside any half-burnt logs as you'll want to use these again. Scrunch up a few pages of newspaper into rough balls and place them in the grate. If you want to use firelighters, you can scrape pieces off them and sprinkle these over the paper balls. Now sprinkle on some kindling, preferably using very dry, thin twigs. If the kindling is damp or unseasoned it won't light properly. Arrange a couple of small, dry, seasoned logs on top and, if there is one, open the damper on the fire to encourage a good draught.

Now it's time to light the fire. Put a match to the balls of newspaper and wait for them to catch. You may have to blow on them for encouragement, or get busy with a pair of bellows if you have such a thing.

It's important to feed the fire, but only when the flames are strong enough not to be extinguished by the logs you're adding. Build up the fire gently until it's doing well, then partially close the damper to stop all the heat escaping up the chimney.

❧ Things to beware of ❧

Never leave an open fire burning in an empty room unless it's protected with a fire guard, otherwise sparks could fly out and start a fire. Equally, you should never leave young children in a room with an open fire, in case they burn themselves.

Something else to avoid is burning wood from the pine family on an open fire because it will spit dramatically as the resin ignites, thereby creating a fire hazard. It will also create a tremendous build-up of soot and burnt resin in the chimney, which will eventually stop the fire drawing and can lead to a chimney fire. If you burn unseasoned pine logs, the chimney will become blocked with thick, impenetrable resin in a surprisingly short time.

It's not a good idea to mix coal and wood in a fire because they combine to create too much heat and lots of clinker that will soon build up in the chimney.

❧ Things to enjoy ❧

There are many things to enjoy with a log fire, including being busy with the toasting fork. You can see pictures in the fire, roast chestnuts on the fender and destroy all sensitive paperwork such as old credit card statements without having to resort to a shredder. In the winter you can burn pine cones, and enjoy the delicious smell from the trimmings of the lavender bushes you've been pruning into shape. If you have a big garden and are burning your own logs, you can also warm yourself with the knowledge that the heat is free and that the carbon your fire is producing is more than offset by the benefits to the environment of growing trees.

Shops often sell bags of kindling, normally at an outrageous price, but really there is no need to buy the stuff if you live anywhere near a green space. Next time you're out for a walk, take a carrier bag with you and pick up all the little twigs and broken branches you see. You'll soon have a decent collection. Leave it to season in a dry, warm place and keep adding to your store. If you're really short of kindling, strips of cardboard are a good substitute.

THE BEST WOODS FOR BURNING INDOORS

What could beat the comfort of sitting in front of a log fire on a chilly day? It's cosy, reassuring and a lot prettier than staring at a radiator. But if it's going to be a pleasure instead of a pain, it helps to choose your logs carefully. Make sure they are well seasoned, which means they should have been left in sunshine and fresh air for at least one year to dry out their sap. The smaller the log, the quicker it will season. If it's unseasoned, or 'green', it won't burn properly and will leach out a lot of sap. This can eventually clog up your chimney or flue, which at best is a nuisance and at worst is dangerous because the chimney can catch fire. Ideally, you should avoid burning conifers ('Scotch' logs in the following poem) because they spit resin. This doesn't matter quite so much in a wood-burning stove but can lead to burnt carpets, or worse, if you've put conifer logs on an open fire. Unseasoned conifer logs can exude so much resin that it will soon fill the chimney with a concrete-like substance.

All woods have a particular calorific value, with some being much higher than others. The higher the calorific value, the hotter the flame. By the way, tradition says you should avoid burning elder unless you don't mind inviting the Devil to come and sit on your chimney. You have been warned!

Another warning is to be wary about what you bring indoors on your logs. No, not the Devil or one of his many helpers, but insect life. You need not worry if the logs are going straight on the fire, but it's another matter if you plan to stack your logs in a decorative fashion near the fireplace or heap them in a large basket. Woodworm, death watch beetle and other unwelcome wood-chewing visitors can all be brought indoors on logs, and will then quickly transfer their affections to your furniture, floorboards or wooden beams. Rather than have to eradicate them when the damage is done, it's best not to bring them indoors in the first place.

This traditional poem tells you everything you need to know about choosing the right firewood.

Logs to burn, logs to burn
Logs to save the coal a turn,
Here's a word to make you wise,
When you hear the woodman's cries.

Never heed his usual tale,
That he has good logs for sale,
But read these lines and really learn,
The proper kind of logs to burn.

Oak logs will warm you well,
If they're old and dry.
Larch logs of pine will smell,
But the sparks will fly.

Beech logs for Christmas time,
Yew logs heat well.
'Scotch' logs it is a crime
For anyone to sell.

Birch logs will burn too fast,
Chestnut scarce at all.
Hawthorn logs are good to last
If you cut them in the fall.

Holly logs will burn like wax,
You should burn them green.
Elm logs like smouldering flax
No flame to be seen.

Pear logs and apple logs,
They will scent your room.
Cherry logs across the dogs
Smell like flowers in bloom.

But ash logs, all smooth and grey,
Burn them green or old;
Buy up all that come your way,
They're worth their weight in gold.

Draught dodging

Y ou don't have to live in the countryside to have a draughty home, but there is definitely something about being surrounded by those wide open spaces that encourages knife-like draughts to creep in under doors and around window frames. Old, timber-framed houses are particularly susceptible to draughts as there can be so many tiny gaps between the timber frame and the lath and plaster walls. Here are some tried and tested country solutions to those draughts.

✎ It's curtains ✎

Of course, it makes sense to have curtains at all your windows so you can close them at night. But have you thought about putting curtains over the front and back doors? The heavier and wider these curtains are, the greater their ability to keep out draughts. You need a special curtain rod, called a portière, which runs across the top of the inner doorframe and swings out when you open the door. This stops you becoming engulfed in swathes of curtain when opening the door, which might be alarming for your visitors. It also prevents you catching your foot in the hem of the curtain and taking a purler down the front path. Alternatively, if space allows, you could put up an ordinary curtain rod (but choose an attractive one) and draw the curtain across the door. You can always take down the curtain in the summer if you wish before putting it back in the autumn.

✎ Sausage dogs ✎

Sometimes draughts whistle under inner doors when they're closed, always managing to catch you in the back of the neck or to freeze your ankles when you're trying to relax. It may not be practical to put up a curtain here but you could make a long sausage to put across the bottom of the door instead. Make sure it's wide enough to cover the whole of the base of the door.

These sausage dogs are so easy to make, and so effective at keeping out draughts, that it's astonishing they aren't used more widely. You can make a very fancy one if you wish, using some lovely fabric (maybe a remnant from those curtains over the front and back doors) and stuffing it with old clothes, more fabric remnants or even rolls of newspaper. For a very quick solution, cut off the leg from a pair of coloured tights (make sure it doesn't have any ladders or holes in it) and stuff it with rolls of newspaper or an old sheet that you've rolled up. Knot the leg at the open end and hey presto! Yes, you'll have to move the sausage whenever you want to open the door, but that's a small price to pay for a warmer room and cosy ankles.

Mothproofing your clothes

If you've ever put on a jumper and stared at the hole that's magically appeared (normally in a prominent place and rarely somewhere that doesn't matter), you will know how annoying it is to share your home with the clothes moth (*Tineola bisselliella*). But what do you do about it?

Prevention is always better than cure, especially as the incidence of the clothes moth is on the rise. Strictly speaking, it isn't the moth itself that does the damage but its larvae, which are laid in the warm, dark snugness of wardrobes and chests of drawers and ravenously chew their way through everything they can find. Rather revoltingly, they like dirty, sweaty clothes, not because of the taste (although, admittedly, they have yet to be questioned about this) but because of the moisture these contain. The larvae are also partial to skin flakes and bits of dried food. Horrid, isn't it? Once they turn into fully fledged moths, they will no longer eat your clothes but they will produce lots of children, which will in turn want to dine on your best togs.

❧ Getting to work ❧

Your first line of defence is to make sure that all the clothes in your wardrobes and chests of drawers are clean. This is especially important at the end of a season, such as when putting away your summer clothes, so give everything a wash before you shove it to the back of your wardrobe or your bottom drawer. Knitted garments are especially delicious for larvae, so you might want to play safe and wrap your best cashmere sweaters in polythene bags (check that these don't have any holes) before stowing them away.

The second line of defence is to clean your wardrobes and chests of drawers by scrubbing at their interiors (especially all the hidden corners) with a damp cloth to remove any eggs. Don't forget to vacuum the floor of the wardrobe afterwards, in case any eggs have fallen on to it. Moths don't like strong smells, so one option is to wipe an essential oil, such as rosemary or tea tree, all over the interior, paying particular attention to the corners.

After this, you can place some scented herbal sachets in the drawers and hang them in your wardrobes, or use blocks of cedar wood sold specially for the purpose (although the oil in these has to be renewed every so often with a special spray). Alternatively, you can go for the old-fashioned option of mothballs, although these have a very telltale smell and contain chemicals that can be dangerous to both humans and animals.

Dry-cleaning will kill any resident eggs or larvae, and also reduce the moisture content of the clothes. Unfortunately, it can also have a detrimental effect on your bank balance, so you might prefer to wrap each garment in a strong plastic bag and leave it in the freezer for a couple of days, after which any resident moth eggs or larvae will no longer be in a fit state to munch on your clothes.

IN THE KITCHEN

Many's the long night I've dreamed of cheese
– toasted, mostly.

TREASURE ISLAND, ROBERT LOUIS STEVENSON

BAKING YOUR OWN BREAD

Once you've mastered the art of baking your own bread, the shop-bought stuff will never taste the same again. Home-made bread has so much more texture and flavour than bought bread, and it's a lot more satisfying. It's cheaper, too! Unlike our ancestors, who had no way of storing their bread, you can bake a big batch and freeze what you don't immediately need. When buying the flour, make sure it is labelled 'strong flour'. This contains more gluten than ordinary flour, which helps the bread to rise. It pays to spend money on good-quality flour, because you will definitely notice the difference when you eat the bread. Of course, you can make the bread in a bread-maker, but the traditional method is to use your hands.

After you've become a confident baker, you can begin to experiment with different flours (add some rye, spelt or a granary-style mixture) and try out some recipes – add a generous handful of porridge oats, sunflower or sesame seeds to a simple wholemeal mixture, or tuck stoned olives or chopped sun-dried tomatoes into the dough of a white loaf just before baking. You can fashion the dough into whatever shape you like. For instance, you can cut up the dough to make rolls, divide it into three sausages that you plait together, shape it into a ball (known as a cob) on a baking sheet or bake it in a loaf tin.

Wholemeal flour on its own can make a rather dense loaf, so you may prefer to begin with a mixture of white and wholemeal flours, as in this recipe.

———•◦•———

Makes 1 large loaf

350 g/12 oz strong wholemeal flour
350 g/12 oz strong white flour
1 tsp sea salt or ½ tsp table salt
1 tsp honey or black treacle
2 tsp dried yeast
Water

———•◦•———

Place the two flours in a large mixing bowl. Put the salt and honey or black treacle in a measuring jug and pour on 150 ml (¹/₄ pint) boiling water. Stir until the salt has dissolved, then top up with cold water until you have 450 ml (16 fl oz) of liquid. Add the dried yeast and stir again, then pour into the flour. With clean hands, start to amalgamate the liquid with the flour until it forms a ball. If it's too sticky, add a sprinkling of flour. If it's too dry, add a tiny dribble of water. Turn out on to a floured board and begin to knead the dough. Squeeze it, push it and manhandle it to activate the gluten; you'll soon build up a rhythm. Continue until the dough is smooth and pliable. Put it back in the mixing bowl, cut a cross into the surface (traditionally said to let the Devil out, but it also helps the dough to rise), cover with a damp tea towel and leave in a warm place for at least one hour or until the dough has doubled in size. If you've got time, you can knock back the dough by punching it, then leave it to prove again. This adds greatly to the flavour and texture of the bread.

When the dough is ready, turn it out on the floured board. Knock all the air out of it by kneading it again, then shape it into a long sausage. Fold this sausage into three, bash it well to knock out any air bubbles, smooth out the joins and place in an oiled 2 lb loaf tin. Cut a slit lengthways in the top of the loaf, cover with the damp cloth and leave to rise again for about 30 minutes. Heat the oven to 210°C/410°F/Gas Mark 7. When the dough is ready, bake the loaf in the oven for 30 minutes or until golden and crusty. Remove the loaf from the tin and knock its base – if it sounds hollow, the loaf is ready. If not, put it back in the oven for a further 7 minutes, then check again. Cool on a wire rack.

If you cut the dough into small rolls that you cook on a baking sheet, bake them for 15–20 minutes, depending on their size. A plaited loaf will take about 30 minutes, as will a cob loaf. If the dough is quite wet, the bread will take longer to cook, so be patient.

THE PERFECT HIGH TEA

Imagine coming home after a long winter's day spent working outdoors. The sun has just set and it's bitterly cold. Your feet have gone numb, your nose glows like Rudolph's and your tummy's rumbling so loudly it sounds like thunder. As you open the back door and take off your wellies, the most delectable aromas waft towards you from the kitchen. Any minute now you'll be sitting round the kitchen table with the rest of the family, tucking into a well-deserved high tea. You can't wait.

Now imagine being in the same frozen state but coming home to afternoon tea, with its dainty sandwiches (preferably with the crusts cut off, and with such thinly sliced bread that you could read the newspaper through it), cake and biscuits, and a pot of tea. To use a gastronomic metaphor, it wouldn't cut the mustard, would it?

High tea originated in the 19th century, when workers would return home ravenously hungry in the late afternoon or early evening, and was an amalgam of afternoon tea and an evening meal. No wonder it was often called a 'meat tea'. It's still a popular meal for children, but lots of adults love it, too. But what does a perfect high tea consist of?

A proper high tea usually begins with something hot, especially in the winter. Depending on the ingredients of this hot dish, it might be followed by scones, cake, biscuits and then, on high days and holidays, the meal can be rounded off by a pudding. It is always washed down with pots and pots of freshly made tea.

Here are lots of suggestions for the perfect high tea that will help to stave off any threat of night starvation. Of course, it's a matter of taste about what you choose to eat but you might draw the line at eating all of it at one sitting. You would also need a very large kitchen table.

❧ The heavyweight hot dishes ❧

- ❧ Shepherd's pie (strictly speaking, this should be made from minced lamb with a mashed potato topping)

- ❧ Cottage pie (again, strictly speaking, this should be made from minced beef with a mashed potato topping)

- ❧ Chicken and mushroom pie

- ❧ Steak and kidney pie

❧ Lighter hot dishes ❧

- ❧ Cauliflower cheese
- ❧ Macaroni cheese

- Fresh ham and fried eggs
- Scotch woodcock (scrambled eggs on toast that has been spread with anchovy paste)
- Welsh rarebit (a thick cheese sauce served on toast and grilled until golden brown)
- Kippers
- Sardines on toast
- Pork or game pie and salad (in summer)

Sweet things

- Fruit scones and jam
- Buttered slices of malt loaf
- Dundee fruit-cake
- Chocolate cake
- Gingerbread
- Parkin
- Macaroons
- Small iced cakes

Puddings

- Sherry trifle
- Fruit jelly
- Apple pie and cream
- Rice pudding

Is this egg fresh?

One of the main reasons for keeping chickens is being able to collect their eggs every day. However, 'collect' is sometimes the operative word because it can take a while to find some of the hens' offerings. And when you do, you may not be sure how fresh they are. So here is an infallible test, based on the fact that fresh eggs contain very little air. The older they are, the bigger the air cell inside them.

Fill a bowl or saucepan with cold water. Carefully lower the egg into the water and watch what happens next. If the egg lies on its side at the bottom of the bowl, it's completely fresh. If the egg stands up and moves around a little, it's not as fresh as it could be but it's still edible. But if the egg floats on the surface of the water, it's very stale and not fit to eat.

Making your own yoghurt

The more you look at the word 'yoghurt' the stranger it becomes. Perhaps one answer is to distract yourself by making your own yoghurt. It's highly nutritious and easy to digest, and you can either eat it in its natural state or flavour it with fruit or honey.

Yoghurt is easy to make yourself, although you do have to ensure it's kept at the right temperature during the fermentation process. You must also ensure that all your equipment is completely clean to avoid introducing any unwanted bacteria to the bacteria you are trying to cultivate. All you need is some fresh milk and a little live yoghurt to act as a starter, plus a container for the fermenting yoghurt – a clean, warmed vacuum flask is ideal – and another for the finished product.

Heat 570 ml (1 pint) of fresh milk to boiling point, then quickly reduce its temperature to 37.7°C (100°F). Stir in 15 ml (1 tbsp) of fresh, live yoghurt, then pour the mixture into the vacuum flask and leave overnight. Alternatively, you can pour the mixture into a covered dish, insulate it with some towels and leave overnight in a warm airing cupboard. If your kitchen is very warm, you may even find that this will provide enough heat. But if you have a dog or cat living with you, make sure that the lid is on tight otherwise they may be the first (and last!) to sample your yoghurt. When the yoghurt is ready, you can pour it into a clean container with an airtight lid and store it in the fridge.

When it's time to make the next batch of yoghurt, you use another 15 ml (1 tbsp) of your current batch as the starter.

PUDDING? YES, PLEASE!

Who can resist a delicious homemade pudding? There's nothing like it. But not every pudding is suitable throughout the year. Some are too heavy for a hot summer's day and others are too light – or cold – for the dead of winter. Here are some ideas for traditional, seasonal puddings to take you through the year. May your waistband never grow tight.

≈ Puddings for spring ≈

Lemon meringue pie
Lemon syllabub
Sussex pond pudding

Cherry tart
Bakewell tart
Rhubarb fool
Pancakes

❧ Puddings for summer ❧

Fresh raspberries and cream
Strawberry tart
Eton mess
Homemade ice cream
Egg custard tart
Apricot tart
Fresh fruit salad
Summer pudding

❧ Puddings for autumn ❧

Apple and blackberry pie
Pears poached in wine
Plum crumble
Baked jam sponge
Treacle tart
Traditional cheesecake
Cranachan

❧ Puddings for winter ❧

Sherry trifle
Chocolate tart
Bread and butter pudding
Rice pudding
Steamed sultana sponge

Spotted dick
Mincemeat and apple tart
Brown bread ice cream

THE CREAMIEST RICE PUDDING

There are times when only comfort food will do. Especially if it's a creamy, sweet rice pudding that's recently come out of the oven, with a golden skin that bursts open to reveal a succulent mixture of milk and rice.

Cook it in a slow oven so the rice has plenty of time to release its starch into the milk. This is not food for those in a hurry. Rice pudding is best made with whole milk rather than semi-skimmed, and if you can find some rich Channel Islands milk then so much the better. If you don't have any pudding rice, you can use short-grain (risotto) rice instead. Soft brown sugar gives a much nicer, rounder flavour than white caster sugar. Don't skimp on the ingredients because a properly made rice pudding is something to treasure, whereas a cheaply and hastily made one can be quite nasty.

Serves 2 greedy or 4 restrained people

45 ml (3 tbsp) pudding or short-grain rice
Scant 45 ml (3 tbsp) light brown soft sugar
570 ml (1 pint) whole milk
Large knob of butter
Fresh nutmeg

Preheat the oven to 135°C/275°F/Gas Mark 1. Spoon the rice and sugar into a wide, shallow casserole dish, add the butter cut into small dice, and grate plenty of nutmeg over the top. Gently pour in the milk and stir well. Place on a baking sheet and slide into the oven. After one hour, remove the dish from the oven and stir the pudding so you incorporate the skin that's forming into the rest of the mixture. This stirring also helps to release the starch in the rice. Return the pudding to the oven and leave for another hour, then check it again. Add a little more milk if it's getting too thick, otherwise give it another stir. Leave for a further hour or until the top is golden brown and most of the milk has been absorbed.

Don't even think about adding sultanas, currants or chocolate to this recipe. Why tinker with perfection?

Boiled fruit-cake

On a chilly winter's afternoon, what could be better than a slice of homemade fruit-cake? Unless it's two slices, perhaps . . . The British have been enjoying fruit-cakes since dried vine fruits were first imported in the 15th century. The cakes were hardly a new idea, though, as the Ancient Romans had made theirs from pomegranate seeds, pine nuts and raisins.

One of the potential snags of baking your own fruit-cake is keeping it in the oven until it starts to dry out, so check it frequently. Boiling the fruit with the butter and sugar makes it wonderfully plump and juicy, and gives it a spicy flavour even though there are no spices in the recipe. The cake is baked in a loaf tin, and if you use a grease-proof cake liner you won't have to grease the tin. Alternatively, bake it in a small round cake tin. As with all fruit-cakes, this tastes better if it's allowed to mature for a couple of days before eating.

175 g (6 oz) butter
110 g (4 oz) dark brown muscovado sugar
50 g (2 oz) currants

50 g (2 oz) sultanas
50 g (2 oz) raisins
50 g (2 oz) mixed peel
100 ml (3½ fl oz) water
225 g (8 oz) plain white flour
5 ml (1 tsp) baking powder
2 medium eggs, beaten

Preheat the oven to 160°C/320°F/Gas Mark 3. Put the butter, sugar, dried fruit, mixed peel and water in a wide saucepan and bring to the boil. Allow to simmer for about 15 minutes until the mixture has become thick and syrupy. It will smell delicious. Leave to cool. When it's tepid, stir in the sifted flour, baking powder and the beaten eggs. Pour into a greased 2 lb loaf tin and bake in the middle of the oven for about 1 hour, or until a skewer inserted into the cake comes out clean (but not too clean). Leave to cool on a wire cake rack.

THE PLOUGHMAN'S LUNCH

Not every so-called traditional dish is old. A ploughman's lunch, which often appears on pub menus with the prefix 'traditional', is typically a hunk of bread, some decent cheese, a blob of sweet pickle and, if you're lucky, a pickled onion. There may be celery, tomato or an apple as well, depending on the generosity of the chef and the time of year. You may think you're eating something that has been enjoyed by farmers and country folk for hundreds of years, but actually the term 'ploughman's lunch' was dreamed up in the 1960s at a meeting of the English Country Cheese Council.

Something to ponder, next time you're having a pub lunch.

Some traditional food and drink

We still eat some foods that have been made in Britain for a very long time, such as parkin. But other foods seem to have gone out of fashion – sometimes, for a good reason. Here is a mixture of traditional British foods. Some of them have fallen out of fashion, some deserve to be revived and some are so familiar that we tend to take them for granted.

✑ Bannocks ✑

A traditional Scottish recipe, bannocks are thin oatcakes that were once cooked on a griddle but are now more usually fried. In his herbal of 1562, William Turner described bannocks as 'Somthyng rysyng in bignes toward the middes, as a litle cake or bannock which is hastely baked upon ye harth'.

✑ Burnt cream ✑

We still eat this delicious pudding in Britain, although now it's more commonly referred to as *crème brûlée* (which is French, of course, for 'burnt cream'). It's been popular for centuries. In 1769, Elizabeth Raffald included the following recipe in *The Experienced English Housekeeper*.

Boil a pint of cream with sugar, and a little lemon peel shred fine, then beat the yolks of six and the whites of four eggs separately; when your cream is cooled, put in your eggs, with a spoonful of orange flower-water, and one of fine flour, set it over the fire, keep stirring it until it is thick, put it into a dish; when it is cold sift a quarter of a pound of sugar all over, hold a hot salamander over it until it is very brown, and looks like a glass plate put over your cream.

By the way, the 'hot salamander' doesn't refer to a warm lizard but to what we know as a hot grill.

Crumpets

These date from Anglo-Saxon times, although they've changed over the years. It was the Victorians who turned what were originally hard pancakes into the soft, spongy round cakes that we know today. They also produced what are now the characteristic holes by putting baking powder into the yeast dough. Their porous texture means they soak up butter in a most delicious way. You can eat them with sweet or savoury toppings.

Faggots

Traditionally, these meaty bundles were a good way of using up pieces of offal, especially after a pig was slaughtered: a conscientious housewife wouldn't have wanted to waste any of it. The minced meat is fried with chopped onion and herbs, then mixed with breadcrumbs and shaped into small rounds that are encased in caul fat before being braised in stock.

Frumenty

This is a very old dish that's been eaten in Britain, as well as Western Europe, for hundreds of years. It's made from boiled cracked wheat, to which a variety of ingredients can be added, including almonds, orange flower water, saffron, currants, eggs and milk. It was once an essential part of the traditional Celtic Christmas feast, but was also a staple dish for Mothering Sunday, when servants were allowed to visit their mothers. The mothers in question would make frumenty, enriched with eggs, to give their children a nutritious treat during the long Lenten fast. It has long since disappeared from our tables into the history books.

❧ Gruel ❧

When Oliver Twist piped up 'Please sir, I want some more' in the Dickens novel of the same name, it was gruel that he was talking about. As gruel is composed chiefly of lots of milk or water in which a very little rice, barley or oatmeal has been cooked, he would doubtless have much preferred a square meal. Today, it is rarely eaten.

❧ Laverbread ❧

This is a traditional, highly nutritious Welsh dish, and it has no connection with bread. It's made from boiled seaweed (traditionally from the Gower peninsula) that's then minced or puréed before being fried with bacon and cockles for a classic Welsh breakfast. It can also be made into laver soup.

❧ Mead ❧

This is a potent alcoholic drink made by fermenting honey and water, and all over the world people have been getting drunk on it for centuries. The word 'mead' comes from the Old English; in *Beowulf* (written some time between the 8th and 11th centuries), the eponymous hero fought Grendel in a mead hall.

❧ Parkin ❧

A soft cake that originated in north Yorkshire, parkin is made from oatmeal, flour, black treacle, golden syrup and ginger. It's rich and satisfying.

❧ Pease pudding ❧

> *Pease pudding hot*
> *Pease pudding cold.*
> *Pease pudding in the pot*
> *Nine days old.*

So runs an old song about what was once a staple dish of north-east England in particular. It's laborious to make, which may be why it's no longer popular. You make it from cooked yellow split peas that are mixed with chopped onion, herbs and beaten egg, and then tied in a muslin bag and boiled for a couple of hours. Traditionally, pease pudding is served with boiled bacon or gammon.

❧ Tripe and onions ❧

This is a classic North Country dish, although it's fallen out of favour in recent years, partly because it's disgusting when made badly and partly because the recent decline of independent butchers' shops has made it difficult to buy tripe. Small pieces of dressed tripe are gently simmered with sliced onions in milk for several hours until they're very soft, and then the sauce is thickened

with butter and flour. Tripe, by the way, is the stomach of a rumi-
nant, such as a cow or sheep.

How to skin a rabbit

Rabbits have long been considered to be 'free' food, with many
country people not averse to eating a rabbit that they've shot or
trapped. Rabbits are one of the traditional quarries of the poacher,
too, and although farmers might be pleased that someone is prepared
to kill off a few bunnies that would otherwise be merrily eating their
way through fields of crops, they may worry about what else the
poacher might take home with him.

Once you've got the rabbit and taken it home, the question arises
of how to prepare it for eating. This isn't a practice for the squeamish,
but generations of women have had to steel themselves to do it in
order to feed their families.

❧ Gutting the rabbit ❧

The first step is to gut the rabbit. This is known as 'paunching'. You
might prefer to do this outside to reduce the potential mess and smell
in your kitchen. Hold the rabbit with its head between your knees,
its stomach facing outwards and its tail facing downwards. Make a
small cut in its stomach with a sharp knife, then pull the skin apart
until its guts are visible. Carefully remove these, making sure you
don't tear them.

❧ Skinning the rabbit ❧

You can take the rabbit indoors at this point. Cut off its four paws
with the sharp knife. Carefully insert your hands into the slit in its
stomach, pushing them between the rabbit's skin and its flesh. Push
them all the way round the flesh until they meet at the back. Now

push the flesh out of the skin, easing the hind legs out of their skin too. Cut off the tail, so the lower portion of the rabbit is completely freed from its skin. Take hold of the two hind legs with one hand and, with the other, pull the skin down the front legs. Sever the tendons holding the skin to the flesh on the legs. Now pull the skin over the rabbit's head, and cut it off.

Finally, you must remove the rest of the rabbit's innards. Cut open its stomach and carefully pull out the heart and lungs (known as the 'lights'), the liver and the anal passage. The rabbit is now ready for the pot.

A WELL STOCKED LARDER

It was the *best* butter.

ALICE IN WONDERLAND, LEWIS CARROLL

THE BEST BITTER ORANGE MARMALADE

Every January, something wonderful happens. Small, bitter Seville oranges briefly appear in the shops before vanishing again. You wouldn't want to eat them raw, with their sour taste and their legions of pips, but they make the most delicious marmalade. What's more, at a time of year after the Christmas festivities when so many of us feel flat (not to mention flat broke), it's magical to fill the kitchen with the nose-tingling tang of oranges. And even better to gloat over the jars of finished marmalade, just waiting for a slice of hot, crisp toast.

You can eat the marmalade as soon as it's cold, but it tastes better for being left a couple of weeks before opening, assuming that you can bear to wait that long. If you buy lots of oranges and then don't have time to do anything with them, you can freeze them whole, then defrost them and turn them into marmalade when it's convenient.

One word of advice, though: you might survey your clutch of glowing jars and think they'll last all year, but unless you're very strong-willed you'll consume them much more quickly than you think. Especially when friends and family hear about the treasure lurking in your larder. Best to make two batches, or even three, just in case . . .

———•·•———

Makes about 4.5 kg (10 lb)

1.4 kg (3 lb) Seville oranges
1 large lemon
3.4 litres (6 pints) water
2.7 kg (6 lb) preserving sugar

———•·•———

Making marmalade is a time-consuming process, so make sure you've set aside several hours, preferably with something good to listen to on the radio. Preparation is important, because everything must be ready when you need it. Ahead of time, make sure you have enough jam jars, either with their own lids or with a packet of the special waxed and cellophane circles sold for jam-making. Wash the jars thoroughly (otherwise the marmalade will go mouldy), drain and stand them on a baking sheet until needed. You can use granulated sugar instead of preserving sugar, but the latter contains more pectin and therefore ensures a better set. Another option is to use one bag of golden granulated sugar instead of preserving sugar, to give a good flavour.

Scrub the oranges and lemon in warm, soapy water and rinse well. Cut in half and squeeze to extract all the juice. As you work, pour the fruit juice into a large preserving pan and tip the pips (as well as any large chunks of membrane) into a bowl. Slice the squeezed oranges and lemons thinly, and place the peel in the preserving pan. Pour the water into the pan. Place the pips in a square of muslin and tie into a bundle, then add this to the pan. Put the pan on the stove and simmer gently for 2 hours, stirring occasionally, until the peel is very soft and the liquid has reduced by about half. At this point, put two saucers in the fridge. Preheat the oven to 140°C/275°F/Gas Mark 1 and put the baking sheet of jam jars in the oven to warm; this sterilises them and stops them cracking when you pour in the hot marmalade.

Remove the muslin bag from the pan, squeezing out all the liquid, and discard. Pour in all the sugar and stir well until it has dissolved, then turn up the heat and bring to the boil. Continue to boil for 15 minutes, remove the pan from the heat, then test for setting point by putting a small dab of marmalade on one of the cold saucers. Let it cool, then draw your fingertip across the marmalade's surface. If it forms a wrinkled skin, the marmalade is set. If not, return it to the heat and boil for another 5 minutes or so before repeating the test. As soon as the marmalade has reached setting point, take it off the heat, stir it and then leave for 15 minutes. Carefully remove the jam jars from the oven. Pour the marmalade into the jars, cover the tops with waxed circles if using, then put on the lids or cellophane circles immediately so a vacuum will form as the marmalade cools. Wipe any drips off the jars and leave to cool, then label. And then eat!

IN A JAM

What could be nicer than some homemade scones, still warm from the oven, smothered with butter (or cream) and home-made strawberry jam? It's tempting to get through a whole jar of the stuff when eaten like this. Once you get into the habit of making your own jam you'll soon find the entire process – from making it to eating it – very addictive. You don't even need massive quantities of fruit, although it's certainly a wonderful way of coping with a glut from your garden.

Generally speaking, the rule for making jam is to use equal quantities of fruit and sugar (always use special preserving sugar because it contains extra pectin to ensure a good set). The quantity of water varies according to the fruit: very juicy fruits (such as strawberries and raspberries) don't need any additional water while others need a little. Here are some recipes for classic jams to get you started.

❧ Dried apricot jam ❧

450 g (1 lb) dried apricots
Juice of 1 lemon
1.3 kg (3 lb) preserving sugar
1.8 litres (3 pints) water

Thoroughly wash the dried apricots, then leave them in a preserving pan with the 1.8 litres (3 pints) cold water to soak overnight. The following day, add the lemon juice and boil for 30 minutes, stirring occasionally. Sterilise the jam jars in a cool oven (see page 190) and place a saucer in the fridge. Pour the sugar into the pan, bring the mixture back to the boil and stir continually to stop the jam sticking. After about 10 minutes, remove the pan from the heat and test the jam to see if it's reached setting point by dropping a small amount on the cold saucer. Leave it to cool and draw your finger along the surface. If a skin forms, the jam has set. If not, return the jam to the heat, bring back to the boil and try again after another 5 minutes. As soon as the jam is ready, take it off the heat and leave for 15 minutes. This prevents the fruit rising to the top of the jars as the jam cools. Stir the jam, pour into the jars and screw on the lids.

❧ Strawberry jam ❧

1.3 kg (3 lb) strawberries
1.3 kg (3 lb) preserving sugar
Juice of 1 lemon
25 g (1 oz) unsalted butter

———•◦•———

Unlike most jam recipes, this involves some preparation, but it's worth it. The day before you want to make the jam, prepare the strawberries by hulling them and checking them for bruises. Discard any that are damaged or too ripe, because these will spoil the jam. Cut up any large strawberries and put all the fruit in the preserving pan. Sprinkle on half the sugar and stir until the fruit is coated with it. Cover the pan and leave in the fridge overnight. The following morning, remove the pan from the fridge and add the rest of the sugar, plus the lemon juice. Stir over a gentle heat until the sugar has dissolved, then bring to the boil. In the meantime, cool a saucer in the fridge and sterilise some clean jam jars by putting them in a cool oven. Boil the strawberry jam hard for at least 15 minutes, then start to test it for setting point (see above). As soon as setting point is reached, remove the pan from the heat, stir in the butter and skim off any scum with a slotted spoon. Leave the jam to settle for 15 minutes, then pot it up in the hot jam jars, cover with waxed circles if using and screw on the lids.

❧ Blackcurrant jam ❧

1.8 kg (4 lb) blackcurrants
2.7 kg (6 lb) preserving sugar
1.8 litres (3 pints) water

———•◦•———

Wash the blackcurrants well, then remove all the stalks and any insects. Place the fruit in a preserving pan and add the water, then bring to the boil. Simmer gently until the blackcurrants are soft and about half the liquid has evaporated. At this point, place a saucer in the fridge and sterilise the jam jars in a cool oven. Add the sugar, bring to the boil and boil for about 10 minutes. Remove the pan from the heat and test the jam for set (see above). When the jam is ready, immediately pour it into the hot jam jars, cover with waxed circles if using and screw on the lids.

How to make rosehip syrup

One of nature's greatest foods may be growing in your garden, or in the nearest hedgerow, without you knowing what to do with it. This is the rosehip, which is the seed pod created by the rose when it's finished flowering for the year. It makes the most delectable syrup, which is high in vitamin C, also has good levels of vitamins A, D and E, and, as an added bonus, is a luscious colour. You can follow generations of country people by eating a spoonful each day for medicinal purposes, or you can combine health protection and gastronomic delight by drizzling it over ice cream, stirring it into yoghurt or putting it on your muesli or porridge. When diluted, it makes a delicious soft drink.

You can use rosehips from any rose bush, although the dog rose (*Rosa canina*) is the traditional choice, but do leave some for the birds (especially if you suspect it will be a cold winter). If you're foraging for hips in the countryside, it makes sense to avoid those growing next to roads because they will be tainted with exhaust fumes. Some people think it's best to pick the hips after the first frosts, when they will be softer.

Be prepared in advance by collecting some smallish glass bottles (with their lids). It's best to use small bottles because the rosehip syrup only keeps for about a week in the fridge once opened.

---

1 kg (2 lb 2 oz) rosehips
1 kg (2 lb 2 oz) caster sugar
Water

Wash the rosehips, remove any stalks and chop the hips into evenly sized pieces. Pour 1.5 litres (2½ pints) of water into a preserving pan and bring to the boil. When it's ready, tip in the hips, bring the mixture back to the boil, then remove from the heat, cover and leave to infuse for at least 30 minutes. Give it a stir every now and then.

At this point, you either need a jelly bag or you can line a colander with a large piece of muslin or, failing that, a clean tea towel that you're willing to sacrifice. Strain the rosehip mixture through the jelly bag or colander into a clean bowl, and leave it until all the liquid has seeped through. Put the juice to one side and tip the rosehip pulp back into the preserving pan, adding another 0.75 litres (1¼ pints) of water. Bring it to the boil, remove from the heat and leave to infuse as before. Strain it again through the jelly bag or colander. You can then repeat the entire process a third time if you wish.

At this point, you must sterilise the bottles by washing them in hot, soapy water, leaving them to drain and then heating them in a cool oven for 15 minutes. Make sure the bottle lids are clean, too.

Wash out the preserving pan, then pour the strained rosehip juice into it and bring to the boil. Keep it simmering until some of the liquid has evaporated, then remove from the heat and stir in the sugar. When it's dissolved, bring it back to the boil and let it boil for 5 minutes.

Remove the bottles from the oven and, using a jug, pour the rosehip syrup into the bottles. Seal with the lids as soon as possible. The rosehip pulp is a good addition to your compost heap.

MAKING YOUR OWN LIQUEURS

⇜ Damson gin ⇝

If you're lucky enough to have a damson tree (*Prunus domestica* subsp. *insititia*) in your garden, or to have access to a fresh supply of these lovely, deep purple fruits, you may be in the happy position of wondering what to do with all that bounty. One option is to make some damson gin. It takes time to mature so you must be patient, but it's delicious when drunk as a liqueur. It's also a splendid Christmas present, assuming that you can bear to give it away. The flavour improves with age so, ideally, you should be highly organised and make this gin a year before you plan to drink it.

———•◦•———

350 g (12 oz) damsons
75 g (3 oz) caster sugar
Few drops of almond essence
1 75 cl bottle of gin

———•◦•———

Prepare a couple of large jam jars (make sure they have decent lids) or Kilner jars by washing them and then sterilising them in a cool oven. Wash the damsons well in warm water, removing any bruised or damaged fruits, plus any insect life that has hitched a ride indoors. Using a darning needle, prick each damson several times, then divide them between the two jars. Now divide the sugar between the jars and top up with the gin. Add a couple of drops of almond essence to each jar. Replace the lids tightly and leave in a cool, dark place. Shake the jars every day until the sugar has dissolved, then allow to mature for at least three months (but no longer than six to avoid the fruit spoiling). At the end of this time, test it for sweetness, adding a little more sugar if necessary. When this extra sugar has dissolved, carefully strain the liquid through a jelly bag and pour the gin into sterilised decorative bottles, then label. The finished gin will keep almost indefinitely, and is best left to mature for a little longer before drinking.

⇌ Sloe gin ⇌

If you don't have any damsons you can use sloes instead, following the recipe above. You can pick sloes from blackthorn bushes (*P. spinosa*) in the hedgerows in the autumn, but take care when doing this because 'thorn' is part of this shrub's name for a very good reason. After you've drained the sloes from the gin, don't throw them away because by now they will have lost their bitter taste. You can coat them in dark chocolate for an after-dinner treat or eat them with ice cream.

BUTTERING UP

If you ever find yourself with masses of fresh milk and equal amounts of spare time, you might like to consider making your own butter. Incidentally, the following method explains why it's so important not to overwhip cream when preparing it for a trifle – because you will have accidentally turned it into butter.

Butter is made from cream, so the first step is to separate the cream from the milk. One method is to pour it into a wide, shallow pan and skim off the cream that rises to the surface of the milk. You can already see that you need a lot of milk to make butter! When you've got enough cream in a separate container, you are ready to start making butter.

Traditionally, butter is made in churns that work the cream backwards and forwards until the fat droplets coagulate. Alternatively, you can place the cream in a jar with a tight lid, and then shake it until it coagulates. At this point, you drain off the liquid (which is buttermilk and makes the most fantastic soda bread). Now pour out the raw butter on to a clean board and begin washing out every trace of buttermilk. To do this, you pour cold water over it and squeeze it, rather like washing a delicate jumper, until all the buttermilk has gone. If you don't get rid of all the buttermilk the butter will soon start to taste rancid. Now squeeze all the water out of the butter. At this point, you can work in some dry salt if you want a salted butter. Taste it to ensure you've got the correct amount of salt. If you've added too much, you can wash it out and start again.

Now comes the exciting part. Squeeze the butter again to make sure you've got rid of all the water, then shape it into oblong blocks and wrap them in clean greaseproof paper. They are now ready to eat.

STORING VEGETABLES

If your vegetable garden has produced all the root vegetables that you wanted, you'll reach a point where you have more than you know what to do with. How can you store them?

≈ Making a clamp ≈

The traditional country method is to make a clamp. This is a heap of soil into which you place all the root vegetables that you want to store, tucked up in a cosy cocoon of straw or bracken. The vegetables in the clamp are less likely to go mouldy or become diseased than if they're kept in a cellar or garage, but they need extra protection in bitterly cold weather and you may have to bring them indoors if there are going to be some severe frosts. When making a clamp, choose a period when there will be a few days of dry weather. Clamps work best when you have plenty of one crop, otherwise if you're storing a mixture you'll have to sift around to find the particular vegetables you want to use.

The first step is to dig up your vegetables, taking as much care as possible to avoid bruising or damaging them. The vegetables that go into the clamp must be perfect, otherwise those with blemishes, bruises, nibbled bits or slug holes will go rotten and infect everything else. Cut off the foliage from carrots, parsnips, swedes, beetroots, celeriac and similar crops, leaving only a small tuft of green.

Brush off the excess mud but don't wash them. Check potatoes for slug damage, and put the affected tubers to one side so you can eat them first. Leave all the vegetables to dry for a few hours.

Now you must choose a suitable site in the garden. It must be somewhere that doesn't collect a lot of water. Dig a trench around the site to encourage any rainwater to drain off the clamp rather than collect in its bottom. Put a layer of straw or bracken on the bottom of the clamp, and arrange the first layer of vegetables on it. Cover it with another layer of straw or bracken (alternatively, you can use sand), then another layer of vegetables. Continue to build up the layers like this, making each one slightly smaller than the last so you create a conical shape. Pile a thick layer of straw or bracken all over the pyramid of vegetables. Push some long pieces of straw through the straw covering to allow moisture to escape. Leave this straw clamp for a few days to let the vegetables sweat, then cover with the earth that you dug out of the trench. Make sure you still have little straws sticking out of the clamp to act as ventilation holes.

≈ Sand boxes ≈

This is an easier option, especially if you want to store lots of different vegetables. You need some wooden boxes (ask for some at your local supermarket or greengrocer) and some bags of sand or coir potting compost. Dig up and check your vegetables as usual, then sort them into types. If the boxes have holes in the bottom or sides, line them with sheets of dry newspaper. Then pour in a layer of sand or compost, followed by a layer of the first type of vegetables. Pour on another layer of sand or compost, followed by more vegetables, and continue until you add the final layer of sand or compost. Be sure to label the box so you know what it contains. Repeat for every type of vegetable you have.

Store the boxes in a cool but frost-free place, such as a garage or shed. Check them every now and then for signs of activity from mice or rats.

❧ Bags of spuds ❧

One of the easiest ways of storing your home-grown potatoes is by putting them in hessian sacks. Don't even think about using plastic bags or sacks because the potatoes will sweat in them and then turn into a smelly, slimy mess. You can buy the hessian sacks from some garden centres or seed catalogues.

Dig up the potatoes and leave them outside to dry. Brush off most of the mud and examine them closely for signs of slugs, eelworms, earwigs, holes where you accidentally speared them with your garden fork, and so on. Put these damaged potatoes to one side. Now, all you do is put the intact potatoes into the hessian sacks. Don't overfill them in case you can't lift them. Store them in a cool place and be prepared to give them a protective covering of sacks or newspaper if the weather gets really cold. Once a month, turn the potatoes out of their bags to check for any that are going off, sprouting or are hatching slugs.

STORING FRUIT

If you're lucky enough to have a glut of home-grown fruit, you'll want to make the most of it. Unfortunately, you can't store it as easily as vegetables, so you need a few options up your sleeve.

❧ Freezing ❧

If you've got the space in your freezer, this is a good place to store your bounty. Soft fruits, such as strawberries and raspberries, will be even softer after they've been defrosted because the ice crystals break down their structure very easily. If that doesn't suit you, you must look for other storage methods. Other soft fruits, such as blackberries, blackcurrants, blueberries and gooseberries, freeze well. Open-freezing is best for these fruits, which means arranging them on a large baking sheet or plastic tray so they aren't touching, and then freezing them as fast as possible. When they're completely frozen, tip them into a plastic bag and seal. When you use them, you'll be able to shake out as many as you want because they won't be stuck together.

❧ Drawers and boxes ❧

If you want to squirrel away some apples or pears for eating during the rest of the autumn and into the winter, you can store them in old wooden drawers or boxes. The traditional method is to wrap each one in a screw of newspaper and then fill a drawer or box with a layer of the fruits and keep it in a cool place. However, you can only do this with perfect fruits, so you've got to check them first for signs of bruising, bird pecks, insect holes and so on. You must also be prepared to keep checking the box or drawer for signs of pests or mould (remember the proverb about one bad apple?).

❧ Bottling ❧

If you don't want to freeze your fruit, you can bottle it. Although this means you must prepare it by gently stewing it in a little sugar and water before putting it in bottles, the bonus is that you have instant puddings (or the instant filling for a crumble) when you open the bottles. Stewed apple is a classic, as is blackberry and apple, but you can also bottle pears, gooseberries and plums. Other fruits, such as cherries, peaches and nectarines, are delicious if you bottle them in a mixture of sugar syrup and brandy. Make sure the jars you use are clean and sterilised, and have proper lids, otherwise the fruit will go mouldy. Don't forget to label each jar with its contents and the date of bottling.

Preserves and jams

Another option is to turn all your soft fruit into jam (see pages 191–4). Again, this involves work but you won't have to buy any jam for months and, depending on how generous you feel, you have lots of potential Christmas presents, too.

Juicing

Stop spending a fortune on shop-bought fruit juices and start making your own. You can experiment with different combinations of fruit if you feel adventurous. The only snag is that you won't be able to keep these juices, but the fact that they're completely fresh is more than adequate compensation.

Puddings and pies

When you're in a hurry or you have unexpected guests, it's such a relief to be able to grab a homemade pudding from the freezer. Soft fruits like raspberries and strawberries may not freeze well in their natural state, but they make wonderful homemade ice creams. You can also put them in pies that you then freeze uncooked – put them straight into a hot oven for perfectly crisp pastry. The list of fruit pies you can freeze uncooked is almost endless.

≈ Drying ≈

One traditional way to preserve apples is to dry them. Invest in an apple-corer that takes out the bits you don't want to eat while keeping the rest of the apple intact. Peel the apples first, then core them and slice into thickish rings. You can thread these on a length of clean string and hang them up in a warm, dry place until they're dry, then store in a sealed plastic bag. Dried apple rings make good snacks if eaten just as they are, or you can rehydrate them by soaking them in a little water or apple juice.

≈ Wine and cider ≈

Finally, you can turn a glut of fruit into wine (see pages 261–3), or make cider (see pages 264–7) from crushed apples or pears (when it's called 'perry').

MAKING BRAWN

When people were largely responsible for producing their own food throughout the year, food was immensely precious and nothing was wasted. When a pig was slaughtered, as many parts of it as possible were converted into food. Even the head was eaten, after being turned into brawn. Here is a recipe for brawn from *The Receipt Book of Elizabeth Raper*, exactly as she wrote it in the mid 1700s.

> Lay the hogs head in cold water all night to soke out the blood the next morning put it in a Kettle and boil it pretty fast till the bones will come out (it should be boiled on fish plate) put it out as whole as you can, and take the bones clean out, then cut and mash it with a Knife, stew in some salt to your tast and when cut enough, put it in a cloth and lay it in a cheese press; let lie all night and the next morning put it in pickle to cover it, made as follows – boil salt and water with a little vinegar and put it in when cold.

CURING PORK

Back in the days when there were no such things as fridges and freezers, it was essential to make sure there would be enough to eat in the winter. That meant slaughtering the livestock in the autumn and preserving it so it would keep over the winter months.

The most effective method for curing pork was to salt it. The pigs were slaughtered in the early autumn, when it was cooler and there was less risk of blowflies laying their eggs on the meat. But eating salted bacon and ham could become very monotonous, so some housewives liked to vary its flavour whenever possible. Here is a recipe for spiced bacon that appeared in *The Art of Curing, Preserving, and Potting all kinds of Meats, Game, and Fish* by 'a Wholesale Curer of Comestibles' in 1864. It gives a fascinating insight into the potential perils of buying spiced bacon in shops and why it was so much safer to spice your own.

Many persons are prejudiced against spiced bacon, *generally* because they may have been deceived in the quality of that purchased at the shops; too often indeed is the spicing resorted to that it may cover defects which would have been too glaring if merely salted. Take a middle of a well-fed large pork, and divide it into pieces that will suit your salting tub; rub them well over, both sides, with warmed treacle, and let them lie for a week, being rubbed and turned every day; then take a mixture of

Bay salt*, beaten fine	3 lb
Saltpetre†, beaten fine	1/4 lb
Allspice, ground	2 oz
Black pepper	1 oz

and rub the meat well with this on the fleshy side only, for a week, after which turn the pieces every other day for a fortnight longer. You may then dry it with cloths, and suspend the meat in a current of air, being turned end for end every third day; and when ready, lay on a nice coat of bran or pollard, and smoke with oak and beech for a fortnight, and finish it by adding peat to your smoking fuel for a week longer. This will be superior bacon.

* Bay salt is large crystals of sea salt that are created when sea water is collected in pits and allowed to evaporate naturally. (The sea salt we know today is dried artificially.)
† Saltpetre is another name for potassium nitrate, which is derived from the earth. It allows meat to retain its red colour during the curing process; without it, the meat would become an unappetising grey.

Preserving Welsh mutton hams

Today, we only tend to eat young lamb, but in the past mutton (an older sheep) was a regular part of the British diet. In the autumn it had to be preserved, in common with all other meat that was destined for the table in the winter and early spring. The following recipe for Welsh mutton comes from *The Art of Curing, Preserving, and Potting all kinds of Meats, Game, and Fish* by 'a Wholesale Curer of Comestibles' in 1864.

Take a couple of legs of prime Welsh mutton, rub them well with treacle made hot, and put them away in a deep pan until the next day. Make a pickle of

Thyme	1 handful
Marjoram	1 handful
Bay leaves	1 handful
Saltpetre	1 oz
Black pepper	2 oz
Bay salt	2 lb
Water	5 pints

boiled an hour and well skimmed, and when cold to be poured over the meat, and to be rubbed every day, and turned for three weeks. Then take them out of the pickle, rub them well in all parts with strong vinegar for one hour, when wipe them dry, and hang them up in a current of air until well dry. Then give them a thorough coat of bran or of oatmeal, and smoke them with

Oak sawdust	2 parts
Peat	1 part
Beech	2 parts
Turfs or fern	1 part

for three weeks or more. Store them in malt cooms and pulverised charcoal, and in three months they will be very good.

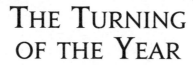

THE TURNING OF THE YEAR

Winter is cold-hearted,
Spring is yea and nay,
Autumn is a weathercock
Blown every way:
Summer days for me
When every leaf is on its tree.

'SUMMER', CHRISTINA ROSSETTI

THE QUARTER DAYS

Not so long ago, the legal year was marked by what are known as the quarter days. These were the four days on which rents became due and magistrates visited outlying districts to settle outstanding legal cases. Even today, some rents are still due on the quarter days.

∽ Lady Day – 25 March ∽

Until 1752, this was the first day of the new year in Britain and its colonies. In the Christian calendar, the 'Lady' in question is the Virgin Mary and the day marks the Feast of the Annunciation (when the Angel Gabriel told Mary she was pregnant with the Son of God). In secular terms, Lady Day marked the beginning and end of the annual contracts between landowners and their tenant farmers. It was therefore a very important day in the year for country dwellers. In the 1600s, hearth tax (payable by anyone whose house was worth more than 20 shillings, and who contributed to the local church and poor rates) was also due on this day.

∽ Midsummer Day – 24 June ∽

This was always popular because it was celebrated with feasting, singing and bonfires. It marks the nativity of St John the Baptist.

∽ Michaelmas – 29 September ∽

This was regarded as the beginning of autumn. It was also a day on which rents were due and accounts had to be paid, so wasn't necessarily something to be welcomed (other than by landlords), even though it was usually marked with the traditional meal of goose. It celebrates the feast of St Michael the Archangel. Hearth tax was once again due on this date.

❧ Christmas – 25 December ❧

Christmas was the time of year when people could have a rest before the hard agricultural work began again. In the Christian calendar, the day marks the birth of Jesus Christ and is one of the major feast days of the year.

❧ And another thing . . . ❧

Each of the quarter days falls close to one of the astronomical turning points of the year: the vernal and autumn equinoxes, and the summer and winter solstices. These are the days on which the sun enters one of the four cardinal signs of Aries, Cancer, Libra and Capricorn. Although we often think of the equinoxes and solstices occurring on a set date each year (as given below), in fact they can vary slightly from year to year because the sun doesn't always enter each sign on exactly the same day.

Vernal equinox – 21 March
Summer solstice – 21 June
Autumn equinox – 21 September
Winter solstice – 21 December

THE TWELVE MONTHS

Here's a different view of the twelve months of the year, courtesy of George Ellis (1753–1815).

Snowy, Flowy, Blowy,
Showery, Flowery, Bowery,
Hoppy, Croppy, Droppy,
Breezy, Sneezy, Freezy.

BRITISH FEAST DAYS

Traditionally, certain days of the year have always been celebrated by eating certain foods. Some of them may seem obvious, but others are more obscure.

∾ Twelfth Night – 5 January ∾

This was always the third of the three big feasts during the Christmas season and was therefore a time of celebration, before all the decorations were removed on 6 January, which is properly called Twelfth Day. For centuries, a rich fruit-cake, called a Twelfth Cake, was always served. It contained a pea or a coin, and whoever found this in his or her slice would be the lord of the household for the evening. Later, in Victorian times, the practice changed and silver trinkets were baked in the cake. The nature of the trinket prophesied the sort of year the recipient could enjoy: a ring indicated marriage, a coin was for wealth, and so on. Today, these trinkets are more likely to be found in the Christmas pudding than in a Twelfth Cake.

∾ Burns Night – 25 January ∾

Originally, this was a special feast day in Scotland, to commemorate the birthday of Robert Burns, who is considered to be the country's greatest poet. Today, it's celebrated all over the world by Scots and non-Scots alike. Although the date has changed (originally, it was the anniversary of Burns' death, on 21 July, that was celebrated), the menu is non-negotiable (unless you're a vegetarian). It celebrates, in the words of the great man himself, 'the great chieftain o' the puddin'-race', which is rather more prosaically known as the haggis. If you're doing Burns Night in style, the haggis is carried in on a splendid dish, followed by a piper. The haggis is addressed, using the words of Burns' own 'Address to a Haggis', and then it's sliced open with a dirk. The Selkirk Grace is recited ('Some hae meat and canna eat, and some wad eat that want it, but we hae meat and we can eat, and sae the Lord be thankit'), and then everyone digs in. The haggis is accompanied by 'neeps and tatties' – swedes and potatoes respectively – and whisky. At the end of the evening, everyone sings 'Auld Lang Syne'.

❧ Collop Monday – Movable feast ❧

This is the Monday of the week in which the Christian fast called Lent begins. In the days when Lent was taken very seriously, it was important to eat up all the perishable food that would be off the menu (such as fats, meat and eggs) during the run-up to Easter. Hence the name of Collop Monday, when everyone ate collops of bacon. The fat from this bacon came in handy the following day.

❧ Shrove Tuesday – Movable feast ❧

Also known as Pancake Day, Shrove Tuesday is the final day for enjoying yourself before you begin your restricted Lenten diet the following day. Traditionally, this is the day for finishing up all your eggs by making pancakes, and frying them in the bacon fat left over from Collop Monday.

✌ Mothering Sunday – Fourth Sunday in Lent ✌

This is an old tradition that dates back to at least the 16th century. It was intended to bring families together during Lent and also to celebrate the role of mothers. An additional benefit of it was that it gave everyone a legitimate opportunity to break their Lenten fast. One traditional food for Mothering Sunday was frumenty (see pages 181–2). Another was simnel cake, which was originally a cake made from fine flour. As the centuries progressed, simnel cake became the traditional cake for Easter Sunday.

✌ Good Friday – Movable feast ✌

This is the Friday before Easter, and marks the day of Christ's crucifixion. In the past, this was a day of complete fasting for many people. Others preferred to eat a little fish. Traditionally, this is the day for eating hot cross buns. After forty days of the most meagre and boring foods (the six Sundays in Lent weren't fast days), the delight gained in eating warm hot cross buns, with their spicy sugariness, must have been quite something.

✌ Easter Day – Movable feast ✌

Lent ends on Easter Saturday, in readiness for the most important day in the Christian church the following day. Today we exchange chocolate eggs, which symbolise renewal, but originally these were ordinary chicken's eggs that were specially painted and decorated for the day. One custom that is peculiar to Britain is eating simnel cake on Easter Day. This is a fruit-cake that contains a thick layer of marzipan and is decorated with another layer of it. It's topped with eleven marzipan balls, to symbolise eleven of the disciples (Judas is excluded).

❧ Lammas Day – 1 August ❧

This was once the start of the harvest, and was celebrated with loaves made by the local farmers from their freshly harvested wheat. Lammas means 'loaf mass', and the loaves were used as Communion bread in the churches. This custom ended with the establishment of the Church of England during the reign of Henry VIII.

❧ Michaelmas Day – 24 September ❧

Michaelmas Day marked the end of the annual harvest and was celebrated with a roast Michaelmas goose.

❧ All Souls' Day – 2 November ❧

This was the day on which everyone remembered the dead. It fell at the end of what was known as Hallowtide, which begins on 31 October with Hallowe'en (All Hallows' Eve). On All Souls' Day, special spiced cakes called soul cakes were baked and given to poor people who would come 'souling' in remembrance of those who had died. The soulers sang songs that varied according to the part of Britain in which they lived.

❧ Martinmas Day – 11 November ❧

The winter months, when nothing grows, were hard times for livestock because there was little food for them to eat. It was therefore a common practice for farmers to slaughter all the livestock that they couldn't feed over the winter, and then to salt down the meat in order to preserve it. This annual slaughtering was carried out in early November (no wonder the Venerable Bede referred to it as Blod Monath, or Blood Month), around the time of the medieval feast of Martinmas. This was everyone's final chance to eat unsalted meat for several months, so it was always a good excuse for a jolly time. Back in the 5th century, Martinmas signalled the start of Advent, which at that point was a six-week fast.

≈ Stir-up Sunday – Last Sunday before Advent ≈

Christmas was the next great feast in the calendar, but everyone had to prepare for it. Part of the preparations involved making the Christmas pudding, which needed plenty of time to mature, and the traditional day on which to do this was the last Sunday before the start of Advent. The day gained its name of Stir-up Sunday from the opening words of the prayer for the day, which begins 'Stir up, we beseech thee, O Lord, the wills of thy faithful people'. Children turned this into 'Stir up, we beseech thee, the pudding in the pot, and when we get home we'll eat the lot'. Everyone in the household had to stir the pudding, always from an easterly to a westerly direction (because the Three Wise Men had come from the east), and make a wish. Silver charms were stirred into the mixture, too, to foretell the future of their recipients on Christmas Day.

≈ Christmas Eve – 24 December ≈

Originally, this was the final fast day of the Advent season, and was observed rigidly. No meat, cheese or eggs were eaten.

≈ Christmas Day – 25 December ≈

For many people, Christmas has replaced Easter as the major celebration of the year, and it's certainly a feast! In the days when Advent was a season for fasting, Christmas Day was a gustatory highpoint after weeks of drearily plain food. The Christmas meal was a lavish affair, featuring a wide selection of meat, poultry and fish for those that could afford it. Mince pies, which featured a pastry Jesus in his crib, were made from a mixture of sweet fruits and minced meat. But Christmas went into a decline during the 17th century when the Puritans succeeded in banning it for several years, and it didn't really recover until Charles Dickens revived it in the 1840s with *A Christmas Carol*. Roast turkey is a relatively modern introduction to the groaning board, on which roast goose was once the centrepiece.

THE SPECIAL DAYS OF THE YEAR

Britain doesn't have many national bank holidays, but many days of the year are considered to be special for a variety of reasons. Here are some, but by no means all, of them.

New Year's Day	1 January	The first day of the new year
Twelfth Night	5 January	Traditionally, a time of great revelry
Twelfth Day	6 January	Christmas decorations come down

Plough Monday	The first Monday after Twelfth Night	Traditionally, the day when farmers returned to work after keeping Christmas
St Hilary's Day	13 January	Traditionally, the coldest day of the year
Burns Night	25 January	A Scottish celebration to mark the birth of Robert Burns in 1721
St Valentine's Day	14 February	A day for sending romantic cards and flowers
Shrove Tuesday	48 days before Easter Day	The last day before the start of Lent
Ash Wednesday	47 days before Easter Day	The first day of Lent
Kissing Friday	38 days before Easter Day	Traditionally, the day when schoolboys could kiss schoolgirls without being punished
Leap Day	29 February	Traditionally, the day when women can propose to men
St David's Day	1 March	The day for the patron saint of Wales
St Piran's Day	5 March	A day celebrated in Cornwall
St Patrick's Day	17 March	The day for the patron saint of Ireland
Spring Equinox	20 or 21 March*	When the day and night are roughly equal in length
Mothering Sunday	Third Sunday in Lent	The day for honouring mothers
Lady Day	25 March	One of the quarter days of the year
Palm Sunday	The Sunday before Easter Day	For Christians, the day when Christ rode into Jerusalem

Maundy Thursday	The Thursday before Easter Day	The day when the monarch gives alms (Maundy money) to the poor
Good Friday	The Friday before Easter Day	For Christians, the day of Christ's crucifixion
Easter Day	The first Sunday after the first full moon following the Spring Equinox	For Christians, the day when Christ rose from the dead
April Fool's Day	1 April	The day when people play tricks on one another
St George's Day	23 April	The day for the patron saint of England
May Day	1 May	Traditionally, a day of great celebration
Oak Apple Day	29 May	Commemorates the restoration of the monarchy in 1660
Father's Day	The third Sunday in June	The day for honouring fathers
Summer Solstice	20 or 21 June*	The longest day of the year
Midsummer Day	24 June	One of the quarter days of the year
Tynwald Day	5 July	A national holiday in the Isle of Man
Swan Upping	Begins on the third Monday in July	The counting of swans in parts of the River Thames
St Swithun's Day	15 July	Traditionally, a test for the next forty days of weather
Lammas Day	1 August	Traditionally, the day when bread was made from the new harvest
Yorkshire Day	1 August	A day of celebration in Yorkshire

Autumn Equinox	21 or 22 September*	When the day and night are roughly equal in length
Michaelmas Day	29 September	One of the quarter days of the year
Trafalgar Day	21 October	Anniversary of the Battle of Trafalgar, during which Admiral Lord Nelson died
Hallowe'en	31 October	The night when ghosts and witches are said to be active
All Saints' Day	1 November	The day when all saints are honoured
All Souls' Day	2 November	The day when all those who have died are remembered
Guy Fawkes' Night	5 November	The anniversary of Guy Fawkes' failed Gunpowder Plot
Remembrance Sunday	Nearest Sunday to 11 November	A time of national remembrance of those who have died in war, marked by a two-minute silence at 11 a.m.
Armistice Day	11 November	The anniversary of the end of the First World War, marked by a two-minute silence at 11 a.m.
St Andrew's Day	30 November	The day for the patron saint of Scotland
Stir-up Sunday	The last Sunday before Advent	The day for making Christmas puddings
Advent Sunday	The first of the four Sundays before Christmas	The start of secular and religious preparations for Christmas
Winter Solstice	20 or 21 December*	The shortest day of the year
Christmas Day	25 December	Christian celebration of the birth of Jesus Christ

| Boxing Day | 26 December | The day when Christmas boxes (gifts of money) were given to servants |

* These days celebrate the ingress of the sun into the appropriate cardinal sign (Aries, Cancer, Libra and Capricorn respectively), and the exact date on which this happens varies from year to year.

BIRTH DAYS

An old rhyme has a lot to say about the day on which we were born.

Monday's child is fair of face,
Tuesday's child is full of grace.
Wednesday's child is full of woe,
Thursday's child has far to go.
Friday's child is loving and giving,
Saturday's child works hard for a living.
But the child that is born on the Sabbath day
Is bonny and bright, good and gay.

TRADITIONS

One for the mouse, one for the crow,
One to rot, one to grow.

TRADITIONAL WAY OF SOWING BEANS

How to Thatch a Roof

Thatched roofs are so wonderfully picturesque, with their beautifully detailed ridges and close-cropped edges. There are more thatched roofs in Britain than in any other European country, so it seems to be a country craft with an assured future.

In the early Middle Ages, when people started to live in villages, they needed an inexpensive way to keep their homes weatherproof, and thatching was a good option. However, because the houses were built so close together, the thatches were a fire hazard and once one caught light, its neighbours were in danger. Today, thatches can be treated with flame retardants but as fires in thatches normally start around the chimney, house owners should make sure that theirs are sound, with no places where hot gases can escape into the thatch and set it smouldering.

If you study a thatched house you will realise that its roof has a steep pitch of at least 45 degrees. That's because the rain that falls on it must run off it quickly before it has a chance to penetrate the layers of thatch and get into the house.

❧ Doing it yourself ❧

If you ever fancy having a go at thatching something yourself, here is what you do. First of all, you must choose the right sort of thatching material, and that means either reed or straw. Traditionally, thatchers used whichever material grew locally, so each area of the country had its own characteristic thatches. Norfolk reed, for instance, was so-named because it was grown on the Norfolk fens and was therefore used as the main thatching material in south-east England. Wheat straw is one of the most prevalent thatching materials, although it doesn't last as long as British reeds. (However, most reeds used in Britain now are imported from other parts of the world and have a shorter lifespan.) Harvesting wheat straw is also more time-consuming than reed.

When using reed, it has to be allowed to dry thoroughly before you use it, because if it's applied while wet it will shrink as it dries. When using straw, on the other hand, it is so brittle that it must be kept wet while it's being worked. Whichever material you use has to be gathered into long, thick bundles. These bundles are then attached in layers, with the first layer laid directly on the roof beams. Each bundle is pegged in place with a giant wooden form of hair grip, known as a spar. When the thatcher has finished securing all the layers, the final decorative ridge is applied. Long straw thatching can then be covered with a fine layer of wire mesh, which looks rather like a huge hairnet, to deter birds from nesting in it.

A thatched roof is a natural form of insulation, keeping the house warm in winter and cool in the summer. When repairs are needed, thatchers usually add more layers to what is already there, which means that very old houses have very thick thatches, with the bottom layer as old as the house itself.

BUILDING A DRY-STONE WALL

In parts of Britain where there is a lot of stone that's easily quarried, it's long been traditional to construct walls from these stones. They are also the ideal type of boundary in parts of the country, such as northern Scotland, where the conditions are too harsh for hedges to flourish.

These walls are called 'dry-stone' because no cement or mortar is used to hold them together. When properly made, dry-stone walls look very beautiful, although they aren't something you can knock up in an afternoon because you've got to spend time fitting the stones together as tightly as possible. A wall of loosely fitting stones will soon fall down. Even a wall of closely fitted stones will need to be repaired every now and then, but if made properly it could last for many hundreds if not thousands of years.

❧ Preparing the site ❧

As with any wall, it's essential to prepare the site properly. It must be cleared of all vegetation, and especially of any saplings or perennial weeds that might try to grow through it. Get rid of tree roots, too, as these will make the site bumpy and uneven. You then dig a narrow foundation trench, so the stones can be bedded into it. Make sure this has a level bottom.

❧ Building the wall ❧

The exact techniques can vary from one area to the next, but in essence they are pretty much the same. You can build a wall that's composed of a single line of boulders (known as a **boulder wall**) or a double line of stones (known as a **double wall**). In each case, you must sort out the stones or boulders into different sizes first, so they are all easily to hand when you need them. Otherwise, you'll waste an awful lot of time scrabbling about looking for the right size stone. You always start off with the largest stones or boulders at the base of the wall, and build up until the smallest stones are on top. If you don't do this, the wall will be top-heavy and precarious.

When building a boulder wall, you place large boulders in a narrow line in the base of the trench and anchor them with small stones. The best boulders are smooth, long and flat. You then build up the wall in layers, making sure they get narrower towards the top.

When building a double wall, you arrange two narrow rows of large stones in the foundation trench, once again anchoring them with smaller stones, then build them up in layers. You tip small stones or rubble into the gap between the two rows. As with the boulder wall, the double wall gets narrower towards the top. Every now and then, you must knit the two rows together by arranging long stones across both rows of the wall. This greatly increases the strength of the wall. When you reach the desired height, the top of the wall is covered with capstones, which span the width of the wall and hold its two rows together.

❧ Openings for livestock ❧

Many of these dry-stone walls were built for fields that enclosed live-stock, so they had to incorporate openings for the animals. Although modern dry-stone walls are likely to contain gates, the traditional opening is a simple gap. Those for sheep consist of a low gap in the bottom of the wall, while those for cattle are complete breaks in the wall. These openings are called 'creeps' in some parts of the country: the low openings are called 'sheep-creeps' and the complete breaks are 'cattle-creeps'. .

TALLY-HO!

'The English country gentleman galloping after a fox – the unspeak-able in full pursuit of the uneatable.' So wrote Oscar Wilde in 1893 in his play *A Woman of No Importance*. At the time, fox-hunting was probably at its zenith, attracting scores of newly middle-class people who longed to prove that they really belonged to the aristocracy.

Although fox-hunting isn't exclusive to Britain, it's long been considered a quintessential part of British life. Some farmers claim that it's one of the best ways of controlling foxes, which are often considered to be vermin capable of doing tremendous damage to livestock. However, fox-hunting with dogs was banned in Scotland in 2002, and in England and Wales in 2004 (coming into force on 18 February 2005). At the time of writing, it's still legal in Northern Ireland.

Fox-hunting is a relatively new sport, because originally people used to hunt deer, which were regarded as a much more noble quarry than the humble, flea-infested red fox. But stag-hunting requires vast tracts of land and these began to disappear as the Industrial Revolution took hold, leading to larger towns, more roads and the coming of the railways.

Hunting is steeped in tradition, and even if today's version of hunting has had to adapt to the legal restrictions placed on it, it still retains its most important links with the past.

✎ The traditional hunt ✎

Before a hunt began, every member of it would gather on horseback at a designated meeting point. This was usually an opportunity for everyone to have an alcoholic drink (traditionally called a 'stirrup cup') before they started the rough and tumble of the hunt. Then the huntsman (the man in charge of the hounds) would blow his horn, signalling the start of the hunt, lead the hounds a short distance and release them to find the scent of the fox. Once they did find it, the dogs would hurtle through the countryside with the hunt following them at full pelt.

When the fox was seen, the cry of 'Tally-ho!' would go up and everyone would pursue the fox. After it was cornered, the hounds would kill it to the accompaniment of more cries, and then various parts of what was left of its anatomy would be handed out among the hunt. The fox's tail, known as the 'brush', was particularly prized and was originally given to the first rider to arrive at the scene of the kill. The fox's paws and head were also awarded as trophies to various riders.

A novice rider, such as a child, taking part in the hunt would traditionally be 'bloodied' after the kill, by having the still-warm blood of the fox smeared on his or her face.

✎ Clothing ✎

Once, it was obligatory to wear a red jacket when out hunting, although this is no longer the case (it depends on the rules of the particular hunt). Despite its colour, the red jacket is called a 'pink'. Huntsmen and huntswomen may wear waistcoats beneath their jackets. The colour of their riding breeches once depended on the hunt to which they belonged, and they wore traditional black riding boots with spurs. It was also traditional to wear a black bowler hat, although many people now wear safety hats or black hunting caps.

SHEEPDOG CALLS

The relationship between a working sheepdog and its master or mistress is one of the greatest examples of the potential connections between dogs and humans. The dogs (which in Britain are traditionally Border Collies) are trained to respond to the farmer's calls so they can herd sheep without frightening or worrying them. The dogs are controlled by the farmer's calls. Here are some of them, although a few can cover a wide variety of instructions.

Away   This tells the sheepdog to move around the sheep in an anticlockwise direction.

Come-bye   This instructs the sheepdog to move around the sheep in a clockwise direction.

Lie down   A variety of meanings, including 'stop' and 'lie down', according to the training that the dog has received.

Look back   The dog must leave the sheep it's working and turn round so it can start to work other sheep.

Stand   The dog must lie down or stop.

Steady   This tells the dog to keep going slowly.

That'll do	This tells the dog that his or her work is finished and it's time to return to the farmer.	
Time now	Another command that tells the dog to keep going slowly.	
Walk up	This tells the sheepdog to walk towards the sheep.	

BRITISH PATRON SAINTS

Britain has a surprising number of patron saints. Here are some of them, and the places, things and people under their patronage.

Date	Saint	Patronage
12 January	Benedict Biscop	Musicians, painters, Sunderland
13 January	Mungo	Glasgow
19 January	Cashel	Cashel
28 January	Glastian	Kinglassie
1 February	Brigid of Kildare	Babies, Ireland, midwives, milkmaids, nuns, poets
3 February	Ia	St Ives (Cornwall)
8 February	Kigwe	Kew (Cornwall)
15 February	Berach	Kilbarry
1 March	David	Poets, vegetarians, Wales
2 March	Chad of Mercia	Astronomers, Lichfield
3 March	Werburgh of Chester	Chester
5 March	Piran	Cornwall, tin-miners
8 March	Duthus	Tain
10 March	Kessog	Lennox
12 March	Mura	Fahan
17 March	Patrick	Excluded people, Ireland, snakes
19 March	Alkmund	Derby
20 March	Cuthbert	Against plague, Durham, Northumbria, sailors
11 April	Guthlac	The Fens
19 April	Alphege	Greenwich, kidnap victims, Solihull

Date	Saint	Patronage
23 April	George	Agricultural workers, England, horses, sheep, shepherds
23 April	Ibar	Begerin
24 April	Ivo	St Ives (Cambridgeshire)
5 May	Hydroc	Lanhydroc
8 May	Odrian	Waterford
25 May	Aldhelm	Malmesbury, musicians, Sherbourne
26 May	Augustine	Canterbury
3 June	Kevin	Blackbirds, Dublin, Glendalough
4 June	Petroc	Cornwall
6 June	Jarlath	Tuam
9 June	Columba	Bookbinders, Ireland, poets, Scotland
16 June	Richard	Sussex
17 June	Nectan	Hartland
11 July	Drostan	Dier
15 July	Swithun	Hampshire, Southwark, the weather, Winchester
16 July	Helier	Ailments of the eyes and skin, Jersey, St Helier
18 July	Theneva	Glasgow
8 August	Ellidius	Hirnant
23 August	Tidfyl	Merthyr Tidfyl
29 August	John the Baptist	Penzance
1 September	Giles	Beggars, blacksmiths, Edinburgh, woods
9 September	Bettelin	Stafford
15 September	Mirin	Paisley, St Mirren football club
25 September	Finbar	Barra, Cork
29 September	Michael the Archangel	Cornwall, grocers, London, police officers, the sick
12 October	Wilfrid	Ripon
13 October	Edward the Confessor	Difficult spouses, kings, separated couples
19 October	Frideswide	England, Oxford, Oxford University
26 October	Cedd	Essex, interpreters, Lastingham
3 November	Winifred	Gwytherin, Holywell, martyrs, Shrewsbury

Date	Saint	Patronage
6 November	Melanie of Rennes	Mullion, St Mellyan
16 November	Margaret	Scotland
20 November	Edmund the Martyr*	Suffolk
27 November	Fergus	Wick
30 November	Andrew	Scotland
4 December	Osmund	Mental illness, paralysis, toothache
6 December	Nicholas	Brides, children, dock workers, grooms, Liverpool, Portsmouth
29 December	Thomas a Becket	Clergy, Exeter College (Oxford), Portsmouth

* Originally the patron saint of England until he was replaced by St George in the 13th century.

WHERE DID ST GEORGE SLAY THE DRAGON?

You might imagine that St George, being the patron saint of England, killed that pesky dragon somewhere in dear old Blighty. On Beachy Head, perhaps, with the waves crashing below him, or on the marshy islands that are now the site of the Houses of Parliament. Actually, no.

There is some folklore claiming that St George slew the dragon in Wiltshire, on the piece of ground where the Uffington White Horse was later carved in the chalk. There is a small area where nothing will grow, because apparently it's been tainted by the dragon's blood. But no, it's not there either.

Tradition has it that St George did his stuff in another part of the world entirely. It is suspected that his story is pre-Christian and that part of it comes from Cappadocia in what was Asia Minor (now modern Turkey). The story is set, however, in Silene (a place that doesn't exist) in Libya. Legend tells us that St George slew a plague-ridden dragon that had taken up residence by the spring in Silene. The dragon was so frightening that no one dared visit the spring to collect the water. The local people tried to pacify the dragon by feeding it a sheep each day. When all the sheep were gone, they had to resort to feeding it their children, which were chosen by drawing lots. One day, the king's daughter was chosen. She was approaching the lake when St George rode by. She begged him to leave her to her fate, but he refused. He made the sign of the Cross and wounded the dragon with his lance, then told the princess to throw her girdle around the dragon's neck and lead it back to Silene with him. The people were terrified at seeing the dragon, but St George told them that if they all converted to Christianity he would slay the dragon for them. The grateful king built a church, dedicated to the Virgin Mary and St George, on the spot where the dragon died. A spring erupted from the altar, its waters able to heal every ailment.

➤ St George's other duties ➤

St George is much in demand. Not only is he the patron saint of England (where his day is 23 April), but also of the following countries and cities:

Aragon	Catalonia	Georgia
Beirut	Ethiopia	Germany
Canada	Ferrara	Gozo
Cappadocia	Genoa	Greece

Istanbul	Moscow	Sicily
Lithuania	Palestine	Slovakia
Malta	Portugal	Slovenia
Modica	Ptuj	Svaty Jur
Moldova	Russia	Venice
Montenegro	Serbia	

He also looks after many different groups of people, including agricultural workers, archers, armourers, boy scouts, horsemen, butchers, knights, shepherds and soldiers. In addition, he is the patron saint of people afflicted with three diseases that still have the power to strike fear in the heart: plague, syphilis and leprosy.

County nicknames

In the days before political correctness loomed large, the inhabitants of some English counties were given nicknames. These were chosen for a variety of reasons, such as a local food or a particular dialect, and some are more complimentary than others.

County	Nickname	Derivation
Bedfordshire	Clanger	After the Bedfordshire Clanger, a form of pie
Cambridgeshire	Cambridgeshire camel or Cambridgeshire crane	After the wildfowl commonly found in the county
Essex	Essex calf	After the famous Essex beef that was once sold in London meat markets
Lincolnshire	Yellowbelly	Believed to originate from the bright yellow waistcoats of the 10th Regiment of Foot (later the Lincolnshire Regiment)
Suffolk	Suffolk fair maids	A compliment to the beautiful women of Suffolk

County	Nickname	Derivation
Surrey	Surrey capon	After the poultry that was bred in the county in the late Middle Ages
Wiltshire	Moonraker	After the smugglers who used to hide their contraband in ponds and then pretend they were raking the water to catch a cheese in it (the reflection of the moon)
Yorkshire	Tyke	After the Yorkshire dialect known as Tyke

TICKLING A TROUT

No, this has nothing to do with keeping an elderly aunt amused on Christmas Day. Instead, it's a venerable and ancient method of catching a fish when you're without reel, line or net. It does mean getting wet, though, so be prepared and don't wear your best clothes.

Before you start, you must observe the local laws about when it's permissible to catch fish and when it isn't. In England and Wales, the open season for trout-fishing is between 1 April and 29 October. In Scotland, it's between 16 March and 5 October. Don't even think about fishing for trout during the rest of the year.

Walk along the banks of a river or stream, looking for signs of trout activity. When you spot something, lie down on your tummy at the point where you saw the trout, and very gently immerse both hands in the water. Hold them apart at first and then gradually bring them together. If you're lucky, you will find you're grasping the fish. Move your hands apart slightly so you've got a firm hold of the fish, then remove it from the water. Throw it back if it's less than 20 cm (8 in) long. The fish will be gasping for air, so put it out of its misery by whacking it on the head with a stone. Leaving it to die from suffocation is cruel.

GARDENING BY THE MOON

There is an old gardening tradition, still practised by some country people, which is known as gardening by the moon. This doesn't mean doing your digging at night, but instead it involves being guided by the moon's phases and by the sign through which it is moving. The biodynamic movement has taken up this form of gardening but it's a long tradition, and one that's well worth following even if you don't adopt all the precepts. People who garden by the moon claim to have higher yields of crops, better-tasting vegetables and fruit, a healthier garden all round, and believe that the crops they harvest for storage keep better.

If you want to start simply, take note of the new and full moons, both of which have a particular effect on plant life, as detailed below. (They have an effect on humans, too, but that's another story.) If you find this works for you, you might like to try the more complex systems of paying attention to the ascending and descending moons, and to the signs through which the moon passes each month. There are further refinements, too, such as noting the aspects that the moon makes to other planets each day.

Anything more than observing the moon's lunations (the new and full moons) will mean either working out all the astrological information yourself or buying a special biodynamic calendar for the year that gives you the most favourable times for all gardening activities.

❧ Waxing moon ❧

The theory is that plants grow in the phase between the new and full moons.

Good for sowing seeds and planting crops
Good for pruning plants in order to encourage their growth

❧ Waning moon ❧

Plants don't grow so much in the phase between the full and new moons.

Good for pruning plants in order to reduce their growth
Good for cutting the lawn if you don't want it to grow again for a while
Good for weeding
The two days immediately before the new moon are good for sowing seeds

❧ Eclipses ❧

Eclipsed new and full moons are times when you can feel justified in putting your feet up and not doing anything in the garden. The energy that eclipses create is so strong that plants react badly to it.

Good for enjoying your garden without working in it
Bad for sowing seeds, planting crops, transplanting, pruning, harvesting and any other activities in which you come into contact with the plants or soil

❧ Ascending moon ❧

This is the two-week phase each month when the moon's orbit is higher than it was the night before. During this phase, the greatest energy is in the part of the plant that's above ground.

Good for taking cuttings

Good for collecting sap from plants

Good for harvesting crops if you want them to be juicy

Bad for pruning plants as they will leach out too much sap

Bad for picking plants for drying as they will be too sappy

❧ Descending moon ❧

This is the two-week phase when the moon's orbit is lower than it was the night before. During this phase, most of the plant's energy is below the ground.

Good for harvesting root crops

Good for pruning and transplanting all plants

Good for stimulating root activity by adding manure to the soil

Good for cutting wood for firewood

❧ The moon and the plant families ❧

Each of the twelve signs of the zodiac belongs to a particular element – fire, earth, air or water. A further refinement of gardening by the moon is the notion that each astrological element is connected to a specific family of plants. You carry out all gardening activities relating to those plants while the moon is in that particular element. If you have to tend them at other times, do so while the moon is in either of the adjoining elements. What you mustn't do is tend them when the moon is in the opposite element to the one that applies to your plants, because this will set them back.

FIRE ELEMENT – ARIES, LEO, SAGITTARIUS

This element relates to all plants that are grown for their seeds. If you're growing flowers purely because you want to dry their seedheads, this is the element in which to tend them. Fire plants include:

All fruits
Tomatoes
Cucumbers
Courgettes, marrows and squashes
Beans
Peppers
Chillies

Opposite element: air

EARTH ELEMENT – TAURUS, VIRGO, CAPRICORN

This element relates to all plants grown for their roots, or whose edible part grows underground. Earth plants include:

Potatoes
Radishes
Onions and garlic
Carrots
Parsnips
All other root vegetables

Opposite element: water

AIR ELEMENT – GEMINI, LIBRA, AQUARIUS

This element relates to all plants grown for their flowers, or where the edible part contains flower buds. Air plants include:

Ornamental flowering plants
Broccoli

Cauliflower

Asparagus

Opposite element: fire

WATER ELEMENT – CANCER, SCORPIO, PISCES

This element relates to all plants grown for their leaves, or where the edible part of the plant is the leaf. Water plants include:

Lettuce and other salad crops

Herbs

Leeks

Opposite element: earth

WELL-DRESSING

In ancient times, people in the Peak District valued their sources of fresh water so highly that they took the trouble to honour them once a year. Local wells and springs were dressed with pictures made from fresh plants and flowers. When Christianity was introduced to Britain, well-dressing was considered to be pagan and was actively discouraged. However, the custom refused to die out and, indeed, it still flourishes in some parts of the country. It is particularly popular in Derbyshire and Staffordshire, although it's now spread to other counties as well. The well-dressing ceremony can take place at any time of the year, but is normally performed in the summer to take advantage of the good weather and plentiful vegetation.

The usual way to dress a well is to make a wooden frame that's soaked in water for several days before being covered in wet clay. Fresh flowers and plants are pressed into the soft clay to form pictures, which are then placed on or near the well.

There are other ways of dressing wells, such as tying ribbons to the branches of overhanging trees. These ribbons float in the breeze and seem to bring life to the air around the well.

HOME REMEDIES

Some home remedies have been handed down through the generations because they really do work. Here are a few that are worth trying, although you should always consult your doctor if you're worried about your health or if the ailment doesn't go away.

≈ Backache ≈

There is a theory that you can cure backache by rubbing a cabbage leaf on the part of your back that hurts. Ideally, you should leave the cabbage leaf next to your skin for a few hours. The only snag with this is that, if you're in a warm room, you will soon start to smell a bit cabbagey. But at least your backache will have gone.

≈ Bruises ≈

Witch hazel is a tried and tested treatment for bruises. Make a cold compress by soaking a pad of cotton wool in the witch hazel, then leaving it on the affected part for as long as possible. Douse the pad with fresh witch hazel whenever it starts to dry out.

Another treatment for bruises is to mash up lots of fresh parsley, then put it on the bruise and hold it in place with a pad of lint and a crêpe bandage. Leave it there for as long as possible. If you don't have any fresh parsley, you can use fresh comfrey instead.

❧ Burns ❧

If you've got a minor burn there are several simple ways to treat it. Always seek proper medical attention for anything more serious.

As soon as you burn yourself, it's important to reduce the temperature of the burnt area. If possible, immerse the affected part in cold water for at least 10 minutes. If that isn't possible, apply a cold compress (a pad of clean linen soaked in cold water) to the area, and reapply it whenever it gets warm.

You now have several options. One is to anoint the affected area with lavender essential oil. This is a marvellous remedy for burns (including sunburn). Another is to make a thick paste of bicarbonate of soda and a little water. Apply it to the burn, cover with a clean pad of fabric (a handkerchief is ideal) and keep it in place with a crêpe bandage. If you have an aloe vera plant, you can cut off one of its leaves and gently rub the juice straight on to the burn.

❧ Colds and flu ❧

Bad colds can be bad news. Other people may tell you it's 'only' a cold, but that is little compensation when your throat has turned to sandpaper, your nose has been rubbed raw, your head is throbbing and you've already used up every hankie in the house and it's still only breakfast time.

One golden rule when treating a cold is to keep drinking lots of fluids. These replace the liquid you're losing through your streaming nose and high temperature, and warm drinks can help to soothe your throat and act as expectorants. Try to eat nutritious foods as they will give your body the materials it needs to recover.

If you're shivery, a cup of ginger tea is warming and comforting. Cut a small piece of root ginger into shreds, boil in a little water for a few minutes, then strain the liquid into a cup. Add a little honey to taste. Ginger is also excellent at combating nausea, which is sometimes a side-effect of colds.

Try eating some raw garlic because it's strongly antibacterial and will give your system a good boost. Some people swear that eating a sandwich made from sliced tomato and raw garlic at the first hint of a cold will soon send it on its way. It may also send everyone around you on their way, but you can't have everything.

If that seems rather drastic, you can make a tea from fresh lemon balm leaves when you first suspect you're coming down with the sniffles. It's also an excellent drink if you've got a feverish cold. Lemon balm tea will help your body to flush out toxins.

Thyme tea is another good remedy, and its antimicrobial qualities will help to chase away all those germs whizzing around inside you. Pick a handful of fresh thyme leaves and steep them in boiling water for a few minutes, then strain and drink. You can also add a few drops of thyme essential oil to a carrier oil and rub this on your chest to soothe respiratory problems. However, you must avoid all forms of thyme as a medical remedy if you're pregnant.

≈ Hair care ≈

A simple way to add shine to dark hair is to steep fresh rosemary leaves in boiling water, strain off the liquid and use it as the final rinse after washing your hair. If you have fair hair, you can use camomile leaves instead.

A simple way to add condition to your hair is to smother it in beaten egg after shampooing it in the normal way. Leave for a few minutes before rinsing it off with warm water. Don't make the water too hot or you'll end up with scrambled egg on your head.

≈ Headache ≈

Assuming that you've now disposed of the cabbage leaf that was combating your backache, all you need to do is to find another one and rub it on the painful bit of your head. This may sound strange (not to mention how it might look to bystanders) but it works.

Another classic remedy, especially for keeping migraines at bay, is to eat one feverfew (*Tanacetum parthenium*) leaf a day. If you have a migraine, it can be alleviated by taking a few drops of feverfew tincture every half-hour. However, feverfew can affect blood clotting rates so you must avoid it if you're on any blood-thinning medication.

✎ Homemade cough mixture ✎

There are many different home remedies for coughs. A simple solution is to eat plenty of grapes, because these act as a natural expectorant. Another option is to mix grape juice with a little honey.

One classic homemade cough remedy sounds disgusting but some people claim that it works on coughs like magic, making them disappear in almost a trice. Peel a medium-sized onion and chop it finely. Spoon some honey into a small bowl and add the chopped onion. Stir it well and leave overnight so the onion juice can mingle with the honey. Take a teaspoonful two or three times a day.

If you've got an annoying cough and you need instant relief, peel a medium-sized onion and blitz it in a blender. Scrape the onion purée into a bowl, add the juice of one lemon and a cup of boiling water. Mix well and add several teaspoons of honey. Take a little of this mixture several times each day.

✎ Painful feet ✎

If your feet hurt, a very old remedy is to slip a comfrey leaf into each shoe. It helps to reduce the pain, especially if you're on your feet all day. As soon as you can get home, soak your feet in a basin of warm water to which you've added a few drops of peppermint essential oil. After drying them, sit with them propped up on a couple of pillows or cushions. Bliss!

READING TEA LEAVES

Ever since tea first came to Britain in the 17th century, people have been reading their tea leaves to find out what the future holds for them. Reading tea leaves – or tasseomancy, to give it its proper name – is one of the easiest forms of divination to practise because all you need is a teapot, some loose tea, and a cup and saucer.

∽ Making the tea ∾

Leave the tea strainer in the kitchen drawer because you need to get as many tea leaves into your cup as possible. Make the pot of tea with some good-quality loose tea, such as Earl Grey, Darjeeling or English Breakfast, and choose a teapot that doesn't have an integral strainer otherwise all the tea leaves will stay in the pot.

You must choose your cup carefully, too, because its shape and colour will affect your ability to read the tea leaves properly. Use a cup with a curved bowl, so the tea leaves can move around it easily. Although cups with patterned bowls can look very attractive, they're hopeless for reading tea leaves because it can be difficult to tell the pattern from the tea leaves. Finally, make sure you use a cup with a handle, as this is an important element in tasseomancy.

∽ Preparing for the reading ∾

After the tea has brewed, you can pour it out in the usual way. Add sugar, milk or lemon as you wish. Tradition says you should only read the leaves of the first cup that's poured out, but you don't have to follow this if you don't want to. There is nothing to stop you reading the leaves in the cups you pour out for other people. If you obsessively read your own leaves they may start to give you misleading or muddled information, so try to restrict your readings to once a day.

Drink your tea while thinking of the question you want to ask the leaves, and only leave a tiny amount of liquid in the bottom of the cup. Now, keeping the question in your mind, turn the cup anti-clockwise three times. Put the saucer over the top of the cup and turn them both upside down. Wait for about a minute, to allow all the tea to drain out of the cup, then turn it up the right way. You're now ready to begin reading the tea leaves.

✑ Looking into the cup ✑

Although it's tempting, try not to rush into the reading. You'll get more out of it if you can take your time, gathering your thoughts, tuning into the energy of the cup and looking at the patterns created by the leaves. Is there only one clump of leaves or are there several? Are you drawn to one clump in particular? Sometimes the leaves create obvious shapes and at other times these seem more random. If you aren't sure about the shapes, it can help to half-close your eyes while looking at them so you see a general outline rather than lots of potentially confusing details. Don't forget to turn the cup in every direction in case you've been looking at something from the wrong angle.

Sometimes, there aren't any tea leaves left in the cup – tradition states that tears have washed them away. On a more positive note, it may simply be that this isn't a good day to give yourself a reading. Try again tomorrow.

✑ Reading the leaves ✑

The position of the leaves within the cup will give you some idea of the time scale to which they refer. Leaves near the rim of the cup refer to the next couple of days; leaves in the middle of the cup describe the next couple of weeks, and leaves at the bottom of the cup refer to events in three or four weeks' time. Leaves near the handle refer to the person who is having the reading.

✑ Interpreting the leaves ✑

It's now time to interpret the shapes formed by the leaves. Sometimes these refer to things in a literal way, and sometimes the shapes are symbolic or even a visual pun. For instance, a circle could mean a ring, such as an engagement or wedding ring, or it might mean a phone call (as in giving someone a ring). An anchor might mean a sea voyage or someone who acts as an anchor, being strong and reliable. Let your imagination and your instincts guide you in the right direction. And have fun!

WASSAIL!

I f anyone ever greets you with a hearty 'Wassail!', the correct way to reply is with an equally hearty 'Drinkhail!' 'Wassail' is a toast, and is the Anglo-Saxon for 'Be of good health'.

⇜ The wassail bowl ⇝

In medieval times, the wassail bowl was a popular feature of Christmas celebrations. It was a communal bowl, often beautifully decorated, filled with a festive alcoholic drink and then passed from one person to the next, each time with the cry 'Wassail!' followed by a kiss. The traditional wassail drink was called 'lamb's wool', consisting of hot ale mixed with spices, sugar and the pulp of roasted apples. In time, the wassail bowl was carried around the streets, too, so that everyone could join in the celebrations. This became a very popular tradition, and it gave rise to several songs, including this one:

Wassail, wassail, out of the milk pail,
Wassail, wassail, as white as my nail,
Wassail, wassail, in snow, frost and hail,
Wassail, wassail, that much doth avail,
Wassail, wassail, that never will fail.

In time, wassailers began to visit houses at Christmas to sing songs, for which they expected to be paid, rather like carol singers today. But wassailing took another form, too.

⇜ Wassailing in orchards ⇝

Gradually, in parts of Britain where there were many apple orchards, such as Kent, Sussex, Herefordshire, Shropshire and the West Country, some people started venturing into those orchards on Twelfth Night (5 January) with a wassail bowl. The idea was to salute and bless the trees with mugs of cider in order to ensure good yields for the coming year. Usually, this involved singing a song as well as other customs, such as leaving food for the trees. For instance, John Aubrey, the 17th-century diarist, wrote of wassailers placing a slice of toast on the roots of each tree.

In time, the orchards were blessed during any of the Twelve Days of Christmas, and some of these wassailings became quite noisy, with gunshots fired into the trees, cakes and bread soaked in cider left in the branches, and cider splashed on the trees or the ground around them. This custom is still practised today, especially in parts of Somerset. The most famous example is in Carhampton, where the wassailing is carried out on 17 January, which is the date of the old Twelfth Night before Britain changed from the Julian to the Gregorian calendar in 1752.

Keeping Christmas

I f you think that too much fuss is made of Christmas and that it's been commercialised almost beyond endurance, you might like to consider that there have been periods in British history when it almost disappeared from view. It was banned completely between 1644 and 1660, during the Puritans' control of England. Christmas was celebrated once again after Charles II gained the throne in 1660, but it went into decline in fashionable society in the late 18th century. Although it might have been celebrated in country districts, the great and the good thought it was a crashing bore. Why bother with it any more? But the tide began to turn in the 1840s, as public sentiment began to react against the sweep of industrialisation and materialism. Prince Albert, who is popularly credited with introducing the Christmas tree to Britain, helped to reawaken the interest in Christmas, but it was the publication of Charles Dickens's short novel, *A Christmas Carol*, in 1843 that really captured the public imagination. Christmas was back!

Even if you don't celebrate Christmas for religious reasons, it's still a special time of year. Most families develop their own ways of doing things, such as opening their presents around the Christmas tree at the stroke of midnight on Christmas Eve or eating grapefruit and sardines for breakfast on the day itself, but the entire festive season has lots of other traditions, too, that have been practised for hundreds of years. Here are some of them.

≈ Advent ≈

The next time you rush to your chocolate Advent calendar only to discover that someone's beaten you to it and scoffed that day's offering, you might like to spare a thought for the Advent seasons of the past. In medieval times, Advent was a time for fasting, before the big Christmas feast. Meat and game were off the menu, although fish was permissible, so most people had to content themselves with surviving on vegetables and lentils during the first three weeks of December. At a time of year when it was cold and dark, this must have been a rather grim experience. Many of the poor, who couldn't even afford to eat a little fish every now and then, literally had a thin time of it. Some were close to starvation.

On Christmas Day, out came the food. Even in the Middle Ages, Christmas was a good excuse for eating your own weight in delectable goodies. The poor might manage to afford a meagre piece of meat, whereas their richer neighbours would really go for broke. What are known as the Twelve Days of Christmas, which run from 25 December to 5 January, were celebrated in style. But no one could stuff themselves silly every single day (although, of course, they could try), so Christmas Day, New Year's Day (1 January) and Twelfth Night (5 January) were the really important feast days.

Villeins, who worked for the local lord of the manor, were excused work during the Twelve Days of Christmas and were invited to a feast provided by their lord. In return, they had to bring gifts, usually consisting of something edible. In some parishes, the villeins were expected to provide all the food for the feast. So the spirit of Scrooge was alive and well, even then.

❧ The Yule log ❧

Fire was very important to our ancestors and had immense significance because it gave them heat and warmth. One of the Christmas traditions, practised especially by landowners, was to prepare a huge

Yule log for burning. Then, on Christmas Eve, the log was dragged home and pushed into the fireplace. Traditionally, it was lit from a small remnant of the previous year's Yule log. If the fireplace was very large, the log might burn throughout the Twelve Days of Christmas, in which case it was considered to be a sign of forthcoming luck. If the fire went out, this was a heart-sinking indication of bad luck to come.

Today, only those of us who live in old houses with large inglenooks have the space to burn a proper Yule log. But many of us have them on our tables instead, in the form of a chocolate Swiss roll covered with chocolate icing.

❧ Father Christmas ❧

As with so many other things, there is a sharp division between the British Father Christmas and the American Santa Claus. Santa Claus arrived in Britain in the 19th century, initially in 1854 when he was mentioned in a story by Susan and Ann Warner called *The Christmas Stocking*, and then in 1863 when Clement Clark Moore's poem, 'A Visit from St Nicholas', was illustrated with the figure of a jolly man. The St Nicholas of the poem had long been associated with Christmas, especially in mainland Europe where he was popularly believed to leave money in children's shoes every 6 December. His Dutch name is Sinterklaas, which gradually became anglicised to Santa Claus. It is often wrongly claimed that Santa's instantly recognisable uniform of a fur-trimmed red suit originated from Coca Cola's Christmas adverts that featured him in the early 1930s. Other illustrations had already depicted Santa in his unmistakable clothes, but the Coca Cola illustrations certainly helped to spread the image of a jolly, bearded, fat fellow in a red suit and matching hat.

Father Christmas, however, has been in existence for a lot longer than Santa Claus. In 1616, Ben Jonson wrote *Christmas His Masque*, which featured a man in long stockings with a tall hat. He then began to appear in other plays and entertainments as well, and became known as Lord Christmas, Sir Christmas and, most popular of all, Father Christmas. He was a very jolly, somewhat pagan figure, often crowned with a wreath of holly and wearing a long green robe, and was frequently treated as a figure of fun. He didn't bring presents; he only gained his sack of toys in the 19th century when his image became melded with that of Santa Claus.

∽ Entertainment ∽

Christmas has always been an important time for entertainment. Today, we slump in front of our television sets or, if we've got the energy, have a trip to the local pantomime. Back in the 14th century, the festive season was enlivened by mummers who travelled around the countryside performing plays. The dialogue for the plays was often passed down from father to son, as not everyone could read and write. The mummers' costumes included masks, which were a wonderful disguise for anyone who wanted to break the law without having to worry about being detected. No wonder these masks were banned in London as well as in various European cities. During Henry VIII's reign, mummers faced three months' imprisonment if they were seen wearing their masks, or 'vizors' as they were then known.

WEEKLY WASHDAY

At one time Monday was always washday, a weekly event marked by harassed women with red arms, mounds of damp washing everywhere and the remains of Sunday's roast being served up cold.

To make matters worse, it was generally considered to be the height of sluttish behaviour if your washing was still hanging outside in the afternoon.

In large families, doing the laundry was a more frequent occurrence. The day of the week that was sacrosanct was Sunday itself, when all good people were supposed to be at church, and certainly not up to their elbows in hot, soapy water. It was, after all, frowned upon to work on the Sabbath. Now, we wash our clothes any day of the week we want. And by machine, too, rather than in a copper, scrubbing them on a washboard with a bar of hard soap and then squeezing all the excess water out of them with the mangle.

The Victorians had a poem about the natural order of washing days.

———•◦•———

They that wash on Monday
Have all the week to dry.
They that wash on Tuesday
Are not so much awry.
They that wash on Wednesday
Are not so much to blame.
They that wash on Thursday
Wash for very shame.
They that wash on Friday
Wash in sorry need.
They that wash on Saturday
Oh they are sluts indeed.

COUNTRY CRAFTS

A man may surely be allowed to take a glass of
wine by his own fireside.

RICHARD BRINSLEY SHERIDAN

Making your own potpourri

In the days before many people practised hygiene and cleanliness, one of the best ways to keep a room smelling sweet was to use some potpourri. This is a collection of scented petals and leaves that gently release their fragrance. Although you can buy bags of potpourri, it's much more satisfying – and considerably cheaper – to make your own. And even better if you can use flowers that you've grown in your own garden.

❧ Wet potpourri ❧

These days, most of us make dry potpourri but our ancestors made what was called wet potpourri. This was made from layers of fragrant flower petals, herb leaves such as lavender and rosemary, spices such as cinnamon and powdered cloves, salt and orris root which 'fixed' the scent. This mixture was placed in special china potpourri jars that had small holes through which the delicious scent would waft to perfume the room.

❧ Dry potpourri ❧

This is called dry potpourri because it's a dry mixture and is made without salt. If you're going to make it, you need to plan it in advance. If you're very organised and want to follow in the footsteps of countless women in the past, you might even consider growing the flowers that you'll later strip to put into the potpourri. These might include classic cottage garden flowers, such as roses, marigolds, hardy geraniums, rosemary, lavender and pansies, as well as fragrant leaves from a myrtle bush, a bay tree and your herb garden. You can add rose hips, cinnamon sticks and dried orange slices, or anything else that appeals to you. You also need some essential oils with which to scent the flowers and leaves, and a fixative that will stop the scent of the oils fading too quickly.

Begin by collecting the flowers and leaves. You might choose them according to their colours, such as only using pink and blue flowers (maybe pink roses and blue lavender for a classic combination), or you might prefer to opt for a complete mixture. Arrange the flower-heads and leaves on a wire rack and leave them to dry in a warm room. Alternatively, you can place them in a very cool oven, with the door left slightly open, but you must watch them closely to make sure they don't go up in smoke. The quicker they dry, the stronger their final colour, but what you don't want is a nice, scorched brown.

Powdered orris root is a traditional choice of fixative, but another option is one of the modern fixatives. Alternatively, you could use chopped orris root or wood shavings. Place your chosen fixative in a large bowl and add a few drops of the essential oils of your choice. Stir them into the fixative, cover with a lid and leave to mature for about four hours.

Place the petals and leaves in a large glass jar (an old-fashioned sweet jar is ideal), and then add the scented fixative. Shake well to mix the fixative with the botanical ingredients before putting on the lid. Leave in a cool, dark place for a week, giving the jar a good shake each day.

The potpourri is now ready. You can tip it into an open bowl or sew it into sachets for your chests of drawers.

Getting hooked on rag rugs

Back in the days when nothing was thrown away and recycling was a way of life, lots of people made their own rugs from old clothes that could no longer be worn. The fabric was cut into strips and these were turned into floor coverings. It was the perfect way of making something from nothing.

There are many different techniques for making rag rugs, according to the sort of design you want to create and your level of ability. One classic method is to plait long strips of cotton together (choosing colours or patterns that go well together) and then to stitch these into a circular or square rug. Alternatively, you can cut long strips of fabric and, using a special rug hook, hook them through some coarse rug canvas. You work from the front of the rug, which allows you to design your own pattern. The intricacy of the pattern is determined by the thickness of the fabric strips – the thinner the strip, the more delicate the design can be. If you're a dab hand with a crochet hook, you can crochet your own rug using thin strips of fabric.

The fact is that, when it comes to rag rugs, pretty much the only limit is your imagination and expertise. Making rag rugs is a world of its own, and it becomes very addictive once you start. Rather than beginning with a full-size rug, it might be better to experiment by making a small pad for a chair or something similar, so you can discover which techniques suit you best.

HAND-DIPPED CANDLES

Candles create a most wonderful atmosphere, and the light they shed is very forgiving to ageing skins. They are also invaluable if you live in a part of the countryside where the electricity supply is a little unreliable at times. So why not make your own? Hand-dipped candles are especially nice and have a very traditional feel. They also make fantastic presents.

It's simple to make candles at home, but you do need some special equipment and you must also abide by all the safety rules to avoid burning yourself (or any innocent bystanders) with hot wax or accidentally letting the wax catch fire because it gets too hot. Never leave children or animals alone with the wax, and never leave the wax on the heat while you go off to do something else. You also need to practise dipping candles, so don't be discouraged if your first efforts aren't very impressive. Give it time.

If you visit a good craft shop you'll be able to buy everything you need. This includes a suitable wax (there is quite a range, including paraffin wax, soy wax and beeswax), some wicks, something in which to melt the wax (a double boiler is perfect), a candle-wax thermometer, plus dyes and fragrances for the wax.

Choose the appropriate wick for the width of the finished candle. You always make two candles at a time, using one long strip of wick. When choosing the length of the wick, don't forget to allow a little extra for the wick that emerges from the top of the candles and joins them together. For instance, if you want to make two 20-cm (8-in) candles you will need a wick that is 40 cm (16 in) long, plus the extra for the top – so it should be roughly 45 cm (18 in) long.

When you're ready, pour hot water into the outer part of the double boiler and put the wax in the inner container. Gently melt the wax but don't let it get too hot in case it catches fire. Stir the wax until it's melted and has reached a temperature of 71°C (160°F). If you want to dye the wax, add the dye to the melted wax and keep testing the colour by placing a small dab of it on a plate and seeing what it looks like when it's cooled. When you're happy with the result, you can add any fragrance that you wish to use. Make sure the wax is still at the desired temperature.

Drape the wick over your index finger so that equal lengths hang down each side of it. Now dip the wicks into the wax. They will need some persuading to go in at first. Hold the wicks in the wax for a few seconds, and then lift them out. Make sure they don't touch one another. Let the wax cool on the wicks for a couple of minutes, then dip them into the wax again. Repeat the process until the candles are the desired thickness. Increase the heat underneath the double boiler until the temperature of the wax reaches 83°C (182°F). Now dip the candles in the wax for a final time, then lift them out and hang them up by their central wick to cool. While they are still fairly soft, trim their bottoms with a sharp knife, then leave them to cool completely. Cut the wick when you're ready to use them.

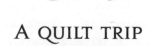

A QUILT TRIP

There is something so cosy about quilts. Whether they feature contemporary patterns or something more traditional, they give instant colour and texture to a room. Antique quilts can cost a lot of money to buy but it's quite simple to make your own, provided that you have the time and patience to do it. Patchwork quilting is a great way of recycling old clothes that can no longer be worn, so you don't have to spend a lot of money on buying all the materials. Quilters often speak of quilting becoming quite addictive, so be prepared for it to take over your life. You can then make your own quilts that will, in time, become family heirlooms. Quilts also make wonderful gifts, not only because of their appearance but because of the love that goes into making them.

❧ Collecting the fabric ❧

If you want to make a patchwork quilt (sometimes known as a pieced quilt), you need to collect lots of fabric first. Ideally, the colours should blend together to give the design some cohesion, but this is entirely a matter of taste. You can reuse old clothes or buy lengths of fabric especially for the quilt. There are many traditional designs that arrange the individual pieces of fabric into specific patterns, such as blocks of four pieces that are then joined to other four-piece blocks to make larger patterns, and blocks of nine pieces that form their own designs.

Start with something that isn't too ambitious, so you can see how you go rather than get bogged down in a design that's too complex for a beginner. Once you've got the hang of these simple patterns you can start to experiment with more complicated designs, such as hexagonal shapes and quite intricate blocks that contain lots of different shapes.

The first steps

When you've chosen the design and fabrics, you make a paper template of your chosen shape for the pieces and use it to cut out the fabric. Alternatively, you can use a special rotary cutter that cuts out many pieces at a time. The next step is to sew the pieces together to make the blocks. Traditionally, of course, this was done by hand but many quilters now use sewing machines, which speeds up the process considerably. It's important to be accurate, though, otherwise your blocks will be slightly different sizes and the discrepancies between the blocks will cause you problems when you piece them together and try to match the seams. It's also important to press each seam with an iron to make it lie flat.

When you've made enough individual blocks, the next step is to sew them together. Again, it's quickest if you use a sewing machine to do this. Make sure the seams are perfectly aligned, otherwise the quilt will start to look messy. Again, you must press the seams open. After this, you make strips to go round the edge of the quilt and stitch them in place.

Assembling the quilt

Hand-made quilts usually consist of three layers: the patchwork pattern, a middle layer of batting that provides warmth (the thicker it is, the warmer it is), and the backing. You arrange these like a sandwich, with the right sides of the patchwork pattern and the backing fabric facing out, and baste them together. You then bind the raw edges with matching fabric, making sure there are no wrinkles in the quilt layers. Finally, you hold the layers of fabric together by stitching them in equal lines. This is what produces the quilted effect.

If you succeed at this and feel like trying something more ambitious, you can make the most beautiful quilts with appliqué work, in which patterns and shapes are stitched on to a single-colour background. Many books give you the patterns and designs of antique quilts, so you can re-create your own without having to spend a fortune on buying them from a shop.

A GLASS OF COUNTRY WINE

If you've ever been faced with a glut of home produce and wondered how you can eat it all or find enough space for it in the freezer, one answer is to turn it into wine. It can take some practice to get into the swing of making decent wine, so don't give up if your first attempts aren't world-shattering. It's very important to be honest with yourself about the results, because these will help you to refine your techniques and learn from your mistakes. Otherwise, your wine will become the equivalent of a social pariah. For instance, if your friends, family and neighbours suddenly remember that they've left something on the stove whenever you offer them your home brew, you might come to the reluctant conclusion that, far from them being forgetful, in fact they have very sharp memories – not to mention taste buds that they want to protect from the worst ravages of your Chateau Country Cottage.

'Country wines', as they're called, can be made from all sorts of fruits, flowers and vegetables, including old socks if some examples are anything to go by. Parsnip is good, damson is rich with a lovely colour and elderflower is champagne-like, but you can also use elderberries, nettles, cowslips, rhubarb, dandelions, plums, peaches, rose hips and a host of other ingredients. And, of course, you can also make your own wine from grapes (in which case it's called 'grape wine'). If you make country wines you need patience to give them time to mature properly, which means waiting for between six and eighteen months before getting out the corkscrew and giving them a taste.

If you're serious about making homemade wine you might be inspired to read a book that goes into the details. You will also need to invest in some specialist equipment, including demijohns, buckets, fermentation locks, sterilising solution, Campden tablets, empty wine bottles and corks. Here, very simply, is what you do, although the exact recipe depends on the ingredients you're using and the quantity you want to make.

❧ Making the wine ❧

Gather the fruits or vegetables and wash them well. Crush or chop the fruit or vegetables to release as much flavour from them as possible and put them in a large white plastic bucket. Pour in some cold water, add a Campden tablet, stir well, cover and leave for 24 hours. Add sugar, yeast and other additives to the mixture, replace the lid and leave in a warm place (21–23°C/70–75°F) for between three and five days. Strain the contents into a sterilised demijohn and, if necessary, top it up with cold water. Fit the airlock to the demijohn and leave it in a warmish place (15–18°C/60–65°F) to bubble away happily until the fermentation process finishes several weeks later. When there are no more bubbles, siphon off the liquid into another clean demijohn, add another Campden tablet, fit the airlock again and leave it for between one and two months. Repeat the process again until the wine is clear of sediment and all fermentation has stopped. You are now ready to decant the wine into clean bottles and securely fit their corks. Leave the bottles upright for about a week, then lay them on their side in a cool place (12°C/55°F) for at least six months for white wine, and at least one year for red. Leaving them longer will probably give you a better-tasting wine, so don't be disheartened if the first bottle tastes a little raw. Leave it to mature and it could turn out to be a winner.

Brewing your own beer

Once you're bitten by the home-brewing bug you will never want to drink certain types of beer again. Real ale, yes. But the mass-produced stuff, no.

If you're new to home-brewing you have two options. You can either start off with a kit to which you only need add water, or you can enlist the help of an expert home-brewer and ask him or her to show you exactly what to do. Even if you decide to take the second option, you would be wise to begin with a simple recipe, as anything too complicated could lead to disappointing results. As with wine-making, you may not get it right at the first attempt, so be prepared to learn as you go along. And take notes of what goes wrong so that, with luck, you won't make the same mistakes again.

You will need some specialist equipment, too, including kettles, barrels and airlocks. As with so many crafts, you can spend lots of money on very sophisticated equipment or opt for something simpler.

✑ Creating your own mixtures and flavours ✑

If you decide to make your own beer from scratch, rather than from a kit, you will need to buy most of the materials from home-brew specialists. These include the fermentable ingredients, such as malts, as well as the hops and yeast that are suitable for the style of beer you want to brew.

When you have all these ingredients, you can consider adding other items to enhance the flavour. This is where things really get interesting because you can have a wonderful time experimenting with everything from chocolate to honey.

❦ The basic process ❦

Home-brewing involves five distinct stages. First, the malted barley is soaked in hot water, which releases the sugars in the malt. The result is called 'sweet wort'. The next stage is to mix the sweet wort with the hops, which produces 'hopped wort'. The best way to do this is to put the hops in a muslin bag or a clean pillowcase, as you will have to remove them again and this saves a lot of time. The third stage involves removing the hops (which is where the pillowcase or muslin comes in so handy) and adding the yeast. During the fourth stage, the yeast is left to ferment. In the fifth stage, you either add sugar or carbon dioxide to the mixture, to increase the carbonation of the beer. The beer is then ready to pour into bottles or kegs, according to the amount you've made and how you want to use it.

MAKING YOUR OWN CIDER

Nature is very bountiful and sometimes she seems to go into overdrive. So what can you do with that avalanche of apples that falls from your trees each autumn and then lies on the grass in reproachful heaps? After you've worn yourself out making apple crumbles, pies and cakes, you could try brewing cider from the apples that are left.

❧ Types of cider ❧

Cider is still a popular drink in Britain, and especially in parts of the country where there's an abundance of orchards. Cider made from apples is simply called 'cider', but if it's made from pears, with no apples at all, it's called 'perry'.

❧ Choosing the apples ❧

You can use any type of apple to make cider, and many people think it works best if you choose a mixture of different varieties, each with its own level of sweetness. Mixing sweet and sour apples creates an interesting depth of flavour, and you can toss in a few crab apples too because they'll contribute plenty of necessary tannin. If you're thinking of planting some apple trees so you can make cider from the fruit in the years to come, consider buying some old varieties from a specialist nursery. Many of these have wonderfully evocative names (how can you resist growing an apple called 'Hoary Morning', or would you prefer 'Braddick Nonpareil'?), as well as a most delicious flavour, and you'll be keeping part of Britain's ancient apple-growing history alive. There are over twelve hundred varieties of native British apple, so there are plenty to choose from.

Ideally, the apples should be left on the ground for a couple of days after they've been picked or they've fallen from their tree, to give them time to soften slightly. Don't worry about sorting out the bruised or damaged apples, or pulling off the apple stalks. This will all be taken care of during the cider-making process.

❧ A pressing matter ❧

The first step is to squeeze all the juice out of the apples, and the best way to do this is with an apple press. You can buy one or make your own, but it must be sturdy because it will be working hard and squeezing a tremendous amount of apples. First, you roughly pulp the apples, either using a specialist piece of equipment called a 'scratter' or a fruit mill, or, if you're processing a small amount, by hand. You then pour some of the resulting pomace on to a large sheet of muslin that's been laid within a frame in the apple press. You fold the rest of the muslin over the pomace to cover it, forming what is called a 'cheese', and then repeat the process with another sheet of muslin. And so it goes on, building up layers of 'cheese' until you've reached the top of the apple press. You then begin to press the cheeses to extract the juice, but you have to do this quite gently to avoid splitting the muslin coverings.

⇛ Fermenting the juice ⇚

The juice pressed out of the cheeses will have collected in a big container below the apple press, and it's now time to allow it to ferment. Cider makers have different ideas about how to do this, with some allowing natural fermentation to take place and others using a variety of yeasts and other additions according to the style of cider they are making. They also add sugar, with the exact amount varying according to the level of sweetness they want to achieve. It's during this fermentation stage that all the debris from the apples, such as the pips, stalks and bits of grass that the apples may have collected while lying on the ground, is cleaned away.

Allowing the cider to ferment but not letting it sit on dead yeast for too long is quite an art, and may take some practice. It has to be drawn off the dead yeast at just the right moment.

≈ Storing the cider ≈

The cider is normally left to ferment for several months before being stored in clean bottles or in a large keg. And this, of course, leads on to the really fun part of the process, which is drinking the stuff.

In Ancient Times

Dark-heaving – boundless, endless, and sublime,
The image of eternity.

Beppo, Lord Byron

ROMAN BRITAIN

When the Romans arrived in Britain they transformed the country. They built roads and created settlements up and down the land. Here is a list of some of the Roman settlements and the towns or cities that they became.

Roman settlement	Modern town/city
Aquae Arnemetiae	Buxton
Aquae Sulis	Bath
Caesaromagus	Chelmsford
Calcaria	Tadcaster
Calleva Atrebatum	Silchester
Camulodunum*	Colchester
Concangis	Chester-le-Street
Coria	Corbridge
Corinium Dobunnorum	Cirencester
Danum	Doncaster
Deva Victrix	Chester
Dubris	Dover
Durnovaria	Dorchester
Durocobrivis	Dunstable

Roman settlement	Modern town/city
Durocornovium	Swindon
Durovernum Cantiacorum	Canterbury
Eboracum	York
Glevum Colonia	Gloucester
Hortonium	Halifax
Isca Augusta	Caerleon
Isca Dumnoniorum	Exeter
Isurium Brigantum	Aldborough
Lactodorum	Towcester
Lagentium	Castleford
Lindinis	Ilchester
Lindum Colonia	Lincoln
Londinium	London
Marnucium	Manchester
Moridunum	Carmarthen
Noviomagus Regnorum	Chichester
Petuaria	Brough-on-Humber
Ratae Corieltauvorum	Leicester
Segontium	Caernarfon
Venta Belgarum	Winchester
Verulamium	St Albans
Viroconium Cornoviorum	Wroxeter

* The first capital of Roman Britain.

HILL FIGURES

There is a long tradition in Britain of carving figures into the chalk hills that dominate southern Britain. Several of these figures have an aura of mystery, with no one knowing exactly when they were carved, or even why. Some of them are located near Celtic hill forts. Is that mere coincidence, or is it a clue to their origins? The jury is still out. Here is a selection of some of the oldest and most interesting figures . . . not to mention one that is quite notorious.

❧ The Long Man of Wilmington, East Sussex ❧

The Long Man holds two staves and stands, legs apart, on Windover Hill apparently looking out at the land around him in East Sussex. He has the distinction of being the largest hill figure in Britain, and therefore one of the largest carved human figures in the world. A sketch drawn in 1799 showed him holding a rake in one hand and a scythe in the other, yet these had vanished by the time another sketch was made of him in 1822. It's not known how old he is, although various theories abound. For instance, he may have first been carved in the Bronze Age or during Roman times. There are numerous theories about who he is and what he is meant to be doing, including suggestions that he's a shepherd looking after his sheep, or that he's a giant who was slain by the giant of nearby Firle Beacon. The Long Man stands near several long barrows, which are Stone Age burial grounds, so another theory is that he's holding open the gates of the underworld.

❧ The Cerne Abbas Giant, Dorset ❧

Who is this man? His state of heightened sexual arousal suggests that he was intended to be a fertility symbol, and certainly women who are struggling to conceive still visit him in the hope that he'll work his magic on them. There are theories that he's a representation of the Roman god, Hercules, because of his resemblance to images of Hercules that have been found in Romano-British archaeological digs in Norfolk. Another theory is that he's a Celtic fertility god called Nodens. What is certain is that on 1 May each year, the sun rises in direct alignment with the giant's phallus. This gives credence to the idea that he's a fertility symbol, but suggests that he was created after the introduction of the Gregorian calendar in Britain in 1752 (when the date switched from Wednesday 2 September to Thursday 14 September, to make up for the lack of synchronisation between the date and the seasons that had been created by the previous, Julian, calendar).

❧ The Uffington White Horse, Oxfordshire ❧

The elongated, rather stylised outline of the White Horse is stretched across White Horse Hill in the Berkshire Downs, near the Neolithic track known as the Ridgeway. It was first mentioned in the 12th century, when it was already considered to be an ancient figure. Research in 1996 dated it between 1400 and 600 BC. One theory is that it's a dragon rather than a horse, because Dragon Hill lies at the foot of White Horse Hill. There's a bald spot, on which nothing will grow, on Dragon Hill, and tradition states that this is where St George slew the dragon (see pages 231–3). The White Horse, therefore, is said to be a depiction of the one ridden by St George. How lovely it would be if this were true! However, the man who is thought to have become St George lived in Asia Minor and never set foot in Britain.

❧ The Westbury White Horse, Wiltshire ❧

There are several white horses cut into the Downs in Wiltshire but this is the oldest. As with all the hill figures, there is confusion about its origins, and this isn't helped by the fact that the steward of Lord Abingdon destroyed the original horse because he didn't like the way it was depicted, and in about 1778 redrew it in a much more representational style but facing in the opposite direction. One theory is that the horse was originally cut into the hillside to celebrate the victory of King Alfred in a battle with the Danes in 878, although there is no hard evidence to back up this claim.

STONE CIRCLES

How many stone circles do you think there are in Britain? And once you've crossed Stonehenge, Avebury and the Rollright Stones off the list, can you think of any others? One glance at the list below will reassure you that there are plenty of them still in Britain.

These stone circles are still shrouded in mystery, even though theories abound about some of them. Some appear to have acted as giant calendars, to help the people of the time keep track of the seasons and celebrate important times of the year. They may also have been important burial places. We may never know exactly but they are all precious and deserve to be preserved. Some are much larger than others, and some are on private land, so you should always check whether a site can be visited before setting off to see it. These ancient stones should always be treated with respect, so that future generations can enjoy them as well.

Aboyne Circle, Aboyne, Aberdeenshire

Appletreewick, near Hebden, North Yorkshire

Arbor Low, Middleton, Derbyshire

Avebury, Wiltshire

Ballymeanoch Standing Stones, near Slockavullin, Argyll

Bamford Moor Circle, Bamford Moor, Derbyshire

Barbrook, near Chatsworth, Derbyshire

Blakeley Raise, near Ennerdale Bridge, Cumbria

Boscawen-Un, St Buryan, Cornwall

Brisworthy Circle, Ringmoor Down, Dartmoor, Devon

Castlehowe Scar, near Shap, Cumbria

Castlerigg, near Keswick, Cumbria

Cullerlie, near Garlogie, Aberdeenshire

Devil's Arrows, near Boroughbridge, North Yorkshire

Druid's Circle, near Ulverston, Cumbria

Eyam Moor, near Grindleford, Derbyshire
Fernworthy Circle, Fernworthy Forest, Dartmoor, Devon
Froggatt Edge, near Chatsworth, Derbyshire
Gamelands Circle, near Orton, Cumbria
Giant's Grave, Kirksanton, Cumbria
Gors Fawr, Mynachlog-ddu, Dyfed
Grey Wethers Circle, near Fernworthy Forest, Dartmoor, Devon
Greycroft Circle, near Seascale, Cumbria
Gwytherin Four Stones, Gwytherin Churchyard, Clwyd
Harold's Stones, Trellech, Gwent
Harwood Dale, Harwood Dale Forest, North Yorkshire
High Bridestones, near Grosmont, North Yorkshire
Hordron Edge Circle, near Ashopton, Derbyshire
Long Meg and her Daughters, near Little Saltkeld, Cumbria
Machrie Moor, near Blackwaterfoot, Arran
Mayburgh Henge, Eamont Bridge, Cumbria
Men-an-Tol, near Tredinnick, Cornwall
Merrivale Circle, Merrivale, Dartmoor, Devon
Midmar Circle, near Echt, Aberdeenshire
Nine Stones Close, near Stanton Moor, Derbyshire
Penrhos Feilw, Holyhead, Anglesey
Ring of Brodgar, Orkney Islands
Rollright Stones, Great and Little Rollright, Oxfordshire
Scorhill, Gidleigh, Dartmoor, Devon
Smelting Hill Circle, near Abney, Derbyshire
Standing Stones of Stenness, Orkney Islands
Stannon Circle, Bodmin Moor, Cornwall
Stanton Drew, near Chew Magna, Somerset
Stanton Moor, near Birchover, Derbyshire
Stonehenge, near Amesbury, Wiltshire
Sunkenkirk Circle, Hallthwaites, Cumbria

Swinside, Swinside Fell, Cumbria

The Hurlers, near Minions, Bodmin Moor, Cornwall

The Merry Maidens, St Buryan, Cornwall

The Nine Ladies, Birchover, Derbyshire

The Nine Maidens of Boskednan, near Tredinnick, Cornwall

The Nine Stones, Winterbourne Abbas, Dorset

Trippet Circle, near Blisland, Cornwall

Yockenthwaite, near Kettlewell, North Yorkshire

IN SEARCH OF KING ARTHUR

Legendary figures abound in Britain, such as Robin Hood and his Merry Men, but one man tops the list – King Arthur. Did he really exist or he is just a good story? Historians have been debating this hot topic for centuries, and they still haven't made up their minds. He's mentioned as being a leader of Post-Roman Britain in a couple of ancient history books, including the 9th-century *Historia Brittonum* (the History of Britain), but that may not be a very reliable source.

According to legend, King Arthur was a great warrior whose court was in Camelot. He was married to the beautiful Guinevere, who betrayed him with Lancelot, one of the twelve knights that belonged to his chivalric order. Arthur was wounded after fighting Mordred at the Battle of Camlann and was taken to the Isle of Avalon, where he is said to be sleeping in a cave until once again he's called upon to lead his people.

Several places in Britain have connections with the legend of King Arthur, although some have a greater claim than others. There is also quite a lot of overlap, with several places considered to be candidates for the original sites of Camelot and Avalon. Here are a few of the places most closely connected with King Arthur and his knights.

❧ Bardsey Island ❧

This tiny island off the Lleyn Peninsula in Gwynedd is thought to be one possible contender for the Isle of Avalon. It's said that Arthur's magician, Merlin, sleeps here in a magical glass castle.

❧ Cadbury Castle ❧

This is a hill fort near Glastonbury that was first built in about 500 BC. Tradition says that it was the site of Arthur's Camelot, and legend has it that Arthur and his knights can be seen and heard riding out from here at the summer solstice and also when the moon is full.

❧ Caerleon ❧

This is a place that crops up repeatedly in Arthurian legend. Is it really the site of his Camelot, as some people believe? There is a stretch of grassy land here called King Arthur's Round Table. Another legend has it that the cave in which Arthur and his men are sleeping is in Caerleon.

❧ Eamont Bridge, Cumbria ❧

The legend of King Arthur isn't confined to south-west England and Wales. The circular earthwork at Eamont Bridge in Cumbria bears the name of King Arthur's Round Table.

❧ Eildon Hills ❧

The Eildon Hills are near Melrose in Scotland, and are one of the (many) contenders for the site of the cave in which Arthur and his knights are sleeping away the centuries, awaiting the call to arms once more.

❧ Glastonbury ❧

This is believed by some to be the location for the Isle of Avalon where Arthur was taken after being wounded in battle. Glastonbury was once called the Isle of Avalon (meaning the Island of Apples) in Welsh, because it was virtually surrounded by water. In the late 1100s, the monks at Glastonbury Abbey claimed to have dug up an enormous coffin with an inscription that said it contained the bones of King Arthur and Guinevere. Some sources said that there were three bodies, the third being that of Mordred. In 1278, the bones were reburied in front of the High Altar in Glastonbury Abbey, in a ceremony attended by Edward I. It's now thought that this was all useful propaganda for Edward I, as well as the Glastonbury monks, and that there were no bones.

Nearby Glastonbury Tor has its own legends, including the story that Joseph of Arimathea (Christ's uncle) founded the first church here. He brought with him the Holy Grail (the chalice from which Christ drank at the Last Supper) and is said to have hidden it in the Chalice Well at the foot of the Tor, where King Arthur and his knights later found it.

❧ Tintagel ❧

According to some, King Arthur was born in the now ruined Tintagel Castle. (Other people claim it was Padstow, also in Cornwall.)

❧ Winchester ❧

A highly decorated medieval table, known as King Arthur's Round Table, is on display in the Great Hall in Winchester. There is no doubt that it's a fake.

Acknowledgements

I loved writing this book and would like to thank everyone at Ebury Press who worked so hard on it, especially Charlotte Cole. Thanks, as well, for all their help to my friend Angela Macpherson for the books she gave me; my tireless agent and friend, Chelsey Fox; and my lovely husband, Bill Martin.

INDEX

I Sing of Brooks, of Blossomes, Birds, and Bowers:
Of April, May, of June, and July-Flowers.
I sing of May-poles, Hock-carts, Wassails, Wakes.,
Of Bride-grooms, Brides, and of their Bridall-cakes.
I write of Youth, of Love, and have Accesse
By these, to sing of cleanly-Wantonnesse.
I sing of Times trans-shifting; and I write
How Roses first came Red, and Lillies White.
I write of Groves, of Twilights, and I sing
The Court of Mab, and of the Faerie-King.
I write of Hell; I sing (and ever shall)
Of Heaven, and hope to have it after all.

Robert Herrick, 'Hesperides'